The Cultural Theorist's Book of Quotations

The Cultural Theorist's Book of Quotations

With Drawings by the Author

Left Coast
Press Inc.

Walnut Creek, California

Left Coast Press is committed to preserving ancient forests and natural resources. We elected to print this title on 30% post consumer recycled paper, processed chlorine free. As a result, for this printing, we have saved:

2 Trees (40' tall and 6-8" diameter)
1 Million BTUs of Total Energy
154 Pounds of Greenhouse Gases
743 Gallons of Wastewater
45 Pounds of Solid Waste

Left Coast Press made this paper choice because our printer, Thomson-Shore, Inc., is a member of Green Press Initiative, a nonprofit program dedicated to supporting authors, publishers, and suppliers in their efforts to reduce their use of fiber obtained from endangered forests.

For more information, visit www.greenpressinitiative.org

Environmental impact estimates were made using the Environmental Defense Paper Calculator. For more information visit: www.papercalculator.org.

LEFT COAST PRESS, INC.
1630 North Main Street, #400
Walnut Creek, CA 94596
http://www.LCoastPress.com

ISBN 978-1-59874-536-8 paperback

Library of Congress Cataloging-in-Publication Data

Berger, Arthur Asa, 1933-
    The cultural theorist's book of quotations / Arthur Asa Berger.
        p. cm.
    ISBN 978-1-59874-536-8 (pbk. : alk. paper)
    1. Culture. 2. Popular culture. I. Title.
    HM623.B46 2010
    306.01—dc22

                    2009049534

Printed in the United States of America

∞™ The paper used in this publication meets the minimum requirements of American National Standard for Information Sciences—Permanence of Paper for Printed Library Materials, ANSI/NISO Z39.48–1992.

10 11 12 13   5 4 3 2 1

CONTENTS

Preface
On Cultural Studies Quotations

Cultural studies, as I understand the term, is an activity that involves using a number of different disciplines and theories to analyze and interpret various aspects of contemporary culture, including the media, popular culture, material culture and everyday life. Thus, cultural studies scholars come from a number of different disciplines and use semiotic theory, psychoanalytic theory, Marxist theory, sociological theory and a number of other theories in their work. These disciplines are needed because we now recognize that texts—the term used in academic discourse for television shows, films, commercials and other subjects and objects of interest—are multi-faceted and generally need to be analyzed and interpreted using many different theories.

I make a distinction between theories and concepts. Theories are wide-ranging and very broad and include many concepts, which are important components of the theory. For example, psychoanalytic theory includes concepts such as the unconscious, the id, the ego, the superego, and the Oedipus complex. When we use a theory in cultural studies, most of the time what we do is apply a concept or several concepts from the theory or concepts from a number of theories, since cultural studies is a multi-disciplinary, pan-disciplinary, and interdisciplinary kind of inquiry and analysis.

The Multi-Disciplinary Nature of Cultural Studies

The term "cultural studies" has been around a long time. One impetus for the development of cultural studies came in 1971 when the Centre for Contemporary Cultural Studies at the University of Birmingham started publishing a journal *Working Papers in Cultural Studies*. It dealt with media, subcultures, popular culture, gender issues and social movements, among other things. Now, most university presses and academic presses directed at scholarly audiences publish books with a cultural studies perspective.

This book of quotations can be looked upon as a way to offer my readers the "best that has been thought and written" (to play upon Matthew Arnold's famous statement) about cultural studies. I've selected those quotations that are, I feel, most useful for readers interested in learning concepts that can be used to do cultural studies. I've refined them down as much as I could without losing the main ideas expressed by the writers.

Some quotes that could be placed in several chapters presented a problem. Should a quote by a Marxist semiotician be placed in the chapter on Marxist theory or semiotic theory? I relied on my sense of where the quote fit best, but it can be seen as a fielder's choice. Another problem I faced was finding quotes that were both short—or relatively short—and substantive. I did the best I could in choosing material that fit those requirements.

This book is a supreme effort in minimalism and reaches the apex (some might say the nadir) of my career as a writer on cultural studies and media criticism. In 1982 I wrote a book, *Media Analysis Techniques* (still in print), that deals with four important theories. In 1995 I wrote *Cultural Criticism: A Primer of Key Concepts* that deals with five theoretical approaches to be used in doing cultural studies. Then ten years later, in 2005, I wrote *Making Sense of Media: Key Texts in Media and Cultural Studies*, that dealt with nineteen books by important cultural theorists. In 2006, I wrote *50 Ways to Understand Communication: A Guided Tour of Key Ideas and Theorists in Communication, Media and Culture.*

And now, with this book, I'm offering three hundred (approximately) short selections, none more than 300 words, on the same topics. My work in this book has been mostly confined to finding selections to use and deciding in which order I should put them. I have written short introductions to each section explaining what its general subject matter deals with, so I've not been completely "left out" of this book. I've also included a few quotations from my own work here and there—mostly charts comparing and contrasting phenomena of interest.

I have not commented on the quotations but am offering what is, in essence, a "guided tour" of the writings of culture critics and media analysts, one of those tours in which you can say, "If I'm on page nineteen, we must be in semiotics-land," or something like that. However, as anyone who has traveled abroad and taken tours knows, tourist guides and tourism guidebooks can often be very useful.

I have taken a few minor liberties with the quotations, and in the interest of economy and readability I have deleted some sentences that were not germane to the argument of the authors. I also have connected some passages that were separated from one another, using ellipses, and I've changed the paragraph structure here and there so the book is easier to read. But I've not altered the content of the messages other than in the relatively superficial the ways I've just described.

Ways of Reading this Book

You can read this book from cover to cover if you wish. It does have a logical organization to it, starting with semiotics and ending with media, an important component of modern societies and cultures. For those who like surprises, it is possible to dip into the book here and there, reading it in a way analogous to the way we often listen to MP3 players—and using the book as what might be described as a cultural studies shuffle.

Millions of people are walking around listening to MP3 players that play the music they have loaded into their players as a shuffle, which can be defined as a random arrangement of songs and music. The shuffle functions in music like a pastiche does in visual art. In a pastiche, bits and pieces of different images are placed together to form some kind of whole. I've made pastiches in which I pasted together images from magazines, material from help wanted ads, drawings I had made, and other kinds of images.

According to many scholars of postmodernism, the pastiche is the iconic example of postmodern art and culture. If this is so, the shuffle reveals itself as a paradigmatic postmodern audio format. Most of the people listening to music arranged as shuffles have never heard the term postmodern, even though they are partaking of a postmodern kind of music appreciation. If McLuhan is correct and the medium actually *is* the message, then we have reason to believe that listening to music in the shuffle format contributes to postmodern sensibilities and lifestyles. For the message of shuffle is that randomness is exciting. You never know what will be coming next which may lead those who prefer the shuffle in their MP3 players to perceive their lives the way they perceive their music.

This book can also be seen as a postmodern work—a pastiche of quotations from writers in a number of different fields, assembled and forming an image—an image of cultural studies as it is refracted through semiotics, psychoanalytic thought, Marxist theory (and consumer culture), feminist theory, postmodernism and the media. Another metaphor would be that the book is like a mosaic and each quotation is like a colored tile. When you put the quotations all together you get a picture. That picture we can describe as cultural studies.

I've suggested that there are two ways to read this book: from the beginning to the end or dipping into it here and there, approximating a shuffle. Let me expand on this second approach to the book, which is similar in nature to the way we function in the world, namely looking here and there and trying this and that. When we look at something our eyes tend to follow its outline and examine certain parts of it in short eye movements called saccades. When we try to do something, we often find ourselves trying one thing and if it doesn't work, trying something else.

Life Is a Shuffle

This metaphor suggests that the MP3 shuffle has important implications for the way we live our lives. McLuhan derives individualism and rational thinking from print's linearity, and I believe that we can see certain lifestyles implicit in the shuffle. Slackers can be seen as shuffle-like persons, living life from day to day with no attempt, in the most extreme cases, to give their lives direction.

This perspective is different from the way many people organize their MP3 players, which is according to the artist or by their albums. So you have a much different sensibility at work with non-shuffle users of MP3 players, and the people who don't use the shuffle impose a certain amount of organization on the way they listen to music. We can say that non-shuffled MP3 players reflect a modernist perspective while shuffled MP3 players are postmodernist.

We can see these two lifestyle arrangements in the chart below.

Shuffle	**Album/Singer**
Postmodern	Modernist
Surprise	Expectation
No logic	Logical
No narrative	Narrative created
Dip in book	Read book by chapters

However you choose to use this book, I believe it will provide you with some of the most important insights into that broad field we know as cultural studies, and I hope it will inspire you to investigate, in more detail, some of the sources I have quoted from. They are all listed in the book. There are hundreds, in some cases thousands, of books and articles on each of the topics

I deal with. What I hope this book will do is stimulate you to explore in more depth some of the topics I deal with and read some of the books from which I quote.

I hope you will also find this book entertaining, in the best sense of the term, because the authors you will be reading are the most important thinkers in their fields and offer ideas that are not only about cultural studies but also about the way we live, think, and relate to one another. Thus, this book will be of use to you in your investigations of cultural studies, but it will also offer you many ideas to think about that will help you better understand your mindset, your experiences, your hopes, your desires and your future.

Semiotic Theory

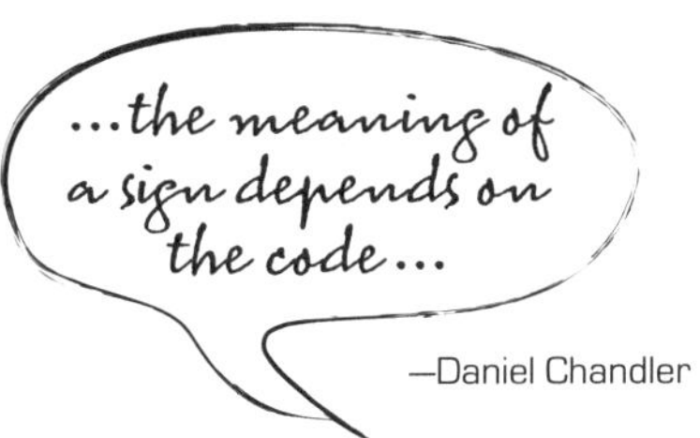

Semiotics is the science of signs—a sign being anything that can be used to stand for something else. Words are signs. So are facial expressions, hairstyles, fashions and just about everything else you can think of. That is, semiotics is an imperialist science that believes that every discipline is really a sub-discipline of semiotics. It focuses upon how people find meaning in various aspects of their lives.

The Greek term *sēmeîon* means sign and is the root for both semiology and semiotics—the two terms used for the sciences that deal with signs. Semiotics has a long history. More than two thousand years ago, Hippocrates, the "father of medicine," (460-377 BC) studied signs and their relation to medical symptoms. Numerous philosophers after him, including Plato, Aristotle, Saint Augustine and Locke, also wrote about signs. But the modern study of semiotics began with the writings of Ferdinand de Saussure and Charles Sanders Peirce. In recent years, numerous scholars have become interested in the subject, and there is a huge literature on semiotic theory and applied semiotics. Peirce wrote that the universe is "perfused" with signs, by which he meant everything is a sign, which means that semiotics becomes a master discipline. That explains why we have social semiotics, political semiotics and many other offshoots of the science.

Semioticians argue that we are always sending messages about ourselves and receiving messages from other people. These messages or "signs" are found in our words, hair colors, body language, facial expressions, fashion styles and everything else we do. How signs work is a complicated matter and is the subject of semiotics. I have selected some of the more important statements written by semioticians to offer you an understanding of what semiotics is about and how it has been used. Semiotics is of interest to people in advertising and marketing as well as psychologists, sociologists and other kinds of social scientists.

I include some writings by the founding fathers of semiotics, the Swiss linguist Ferdinand de Saussure and the American philosopher Charles Sanders Peirce, and some of the more outstanding users of semiotics such as the French critic Roland Barthes and the Italian semiotician, literary theorist and novelist Umberto Eco. What you will discover is that everyone is a practicing semiotician, even if they have never heard the word "semiotics" before. When we "read" people, when we read detective novels, we are functioning as amateur semioticians. What I hope to do with the material in this section is turn amateur semioticians into more professional ones. I have written a book on the subject, *Signs in Contemporary Culture: An Introduction to Semiotics*, and have written a study of American culture, *Bloom's Morning*, that is semiotic in nature.

Language is a system of signs that express ideas, and is therefore comparable to a system of writing, the alphabet of deaf-mutes, military signals, etc. But it is the most important of all these systems. *A science that studies the life of signs within society* is conceivable; it would be part of social-psychology and consequently of general psychology. I shall call it *semiology* (from

Greek *sēmîon* "sign"). Semiology would show what constitutes signs, what laws govern them.

Ferdinand de Saussure

A Course in General Linguistics. New York: McGraw-Hill. 1915/1966.

Concepts are purely differential and defined not by their positive characteristics but negatively by their relations with other terms of the system…. Signs function, then, not through their intrinsic value but through their relative position.

Ferdinand de Saussure

A Course in General Linguistics. New York: McGraw-Hill. 1915/1966.

C.S. Peirce

Every sign is determined by its object, either first, by partaking in the characters of the object, when I call a sign an *Icon*; secondly, by being really and in its individual existence connected with the individual object, when I call the sign an *Index*; thirdly, by more or less certainty that it will be interpreted as denoting the object, in consequence of a habit (which term I use as including a natural disposition), when I call the sign a *Symbol*.

C.S. Peirce

Quoted in J. J. Zeyman, "Pierce's Theory of Signs," in T. S. Sebeok, ed. *A Perfusion of Signs.* Bloomington: Indiana University Press. 1977.

It seems a strange thing, when one comes to ponder over it, that a sign should leave its interpreter to supply part of its meaning; but the explanation of the phenomenon lies in the fact that the entire universe—not merely the universe of existents, but all that wider universe, embracing the universe of existents, as a part, the universe which we are all accustomed to refer to as "the truth"—that all this universe is perfused with signs, if it is not composed exclusively of signs.

C.S. Peirce
Epigraph in T. Sebeok. *A Perfusion of Signs.* Bloomington: Indiana University Press. 1977.

Everything we do sends messages about us in a variety of codes, semiologists contend. We are also on the receiving end of innumerable messages encoded in music, gestures, foods, rituals, books, movies, or advertisements. Yet we seldom realize that we have received such messages and would have trouble explaining the rules under which they operate.

Maya Pines
"How They Know What You Really Mean," *San Francisco Chronicle,* Oct. 13, 1982.

The basic unit of semiotics is the *sign* defined conceptually as something that stands for something else, and, more technically, as a spoken or written word, a drawn figure, or a material object unified in the mind with a particular cultural concept. The sign is this unity of word-object, known as a *signifier* with a corresponding, culturally prescribed content or meaning, known as a *signified.* Thus our minds attach the word "dog," or the drawn figure of a "dog," as a signifier to the idea of a "dog," that is, a domesticated canine species possessing certain behavioral characteristics. If we came from a culture that did not possess dogs in daily life, however unlikely, we would not know what the signifier "dog" means... .When dealing with objects that are signifiers of certain concepts, cultural meanings, or ideologies of belief, we can consider them not only as "signs," but *sign vehicles.* Signifying objects carry meanings with them.

Mark Gottdiener

The Theming of America: Dreams, Visions and Commercial Spaces. Boulder, CO: Westview Press. 1996.

Semiotics is concerned with everything that can be taken as a sign. A sign is everything which can be taken as significantly substituting for something else. This something else does not necessarily have to exist or to actually be somewhere at the moment in which a sign stands for it. Thus semiotics is in principle the discipline studying everything which can be used in order to lie. If something cannot be used to tell a lie, conversely it cannot be used to tell the truth; it cannot be used "to tell" at all.

Umberto Eco

A Theory of Semiotics. Bloomington: Indiana University Press. 1976.

The underlying argument behind the semiotic approach is that, since all cultural objects convey meaning, and all cultural practices depend on meaning, they must make use of signs; and in so far as they do, they must work like language works, and be amenable to an analysis which basically makes use of Saussure's linguistic concepts…his idea of underlying codes and structures, and the arbitrary nature of the sign. Thus, when in his collection of essays, *Mythologies* (1972), the French critic Roland Barthes, studies "The world of wresting," "soap powders and detergents," "The Face of Greta Garbo," or "The *Blue Guides* to Europe," he brought a semiotic approach to bear on "reading" popular culture, treating these activities and objects as signs, as a language through which meaning is communicated.

Stuart Hall, ed.

Representation: Cultural Representations and Signifying Practices. London: Sage Publications. 1997.

I have suggested that tourist attractions are signs.... Sightseers do not, in any empirical sense, see San Francisco. They see Fisherman's Wharf, a cable car, the Golden Gate Bridge, Union Square, Coit Tower, the Presidio, City Lights Bookstore, Chinatown, and perhaps the Haight Ashbury or a nude go-go dancer in a North Beach-Barbary Coast club.

Dean MacCannell

The Tourist: A New Theory of the Leisure Class. New York: Schocken Books. 1976.

The quotidian is what is humble and solid, what is taken for granted and that of which all the parts follow each other in such a regular, unvarying succession that those concerned have no call to question their sequence; thus it is undated and (apparently) insignificant.

Henri Lefebvre

Everyday Life in the Modern World. Trans. Sacha Rabinovich. New Brunswick, NJ: Transaction Publications. 1984.

If you allow the swarms of signs to flow over you from television and radio sets, from films and newspaper and ratify the commentaries that determine their meanings, you will become the passive victim of the situation; but insert a distinction or two—for instance everyday life and modernity—and the situation is changed: you are now an active interpreter of signs.

Henri Lefebvre

Everyday Life in the Modern World. Trans. Sacha Rabinovich. New Brunswick, NJ: Transaction Publications. 1984.

There are two reasons why semiology is a vital area of study for the aesthetics of film. First, any criticism necessarily depends upon knowing what a text means, being able to read it. Unless we understand the code or mode of expression which permits meaning to exist in the cinema, we are condemned to massive imprecision and nebulosity in film criticism, an unfounded reliance on intuition and momentary impressions. Secondly, it is becoming increasingly evident that any definition of art must be made as part of a theory of semiology.... The whole drift of modern thought about the arts has been to submerge them in general theories of communication, whether psychological or sociological, to treat works of art like any other text or message and to deny them any specific aesthetic qualities by which they can be distinguished, except of the most banal kind.

Peter Wollen

Signs and Meaning in the Cinema. Bloomington: Indiana University Press. 1972.

Every image on the screen is a sign, that is, it has meaning, it carries information. This meaning, however, can be of two kinds. On the one hand, images on the screen reproduce some sorts of objects of the real world. A semantic relationship is established between these objects and the screen images. The objects become the meanings of the images reproduced on the screen. On the other hand, the images on the screen may be augmented by some additional, often totally unexpected meanings. Lighting, montage, interplay of depth levels, changes of speed, etc. may impart to the objects additional meanings—symbolic, metaphorical, metonymical, etc.

Yuri Lotman

Semiotics of Cinema. Trans. Mark E. Suino. Ann Arbor: Michigan Slavic Contributions. 1976.

The question may arise: how can we reconcile cinematography having great semiotic complexity with the requirements of accessibility and comprehension to a wide segment of viewers having varying degrees of preparation. By its very nature, after all, cinema is a mass medium...film is a multi-layered structure, and its layers are organized with unequal degrees of complexity. The audience, having various degrees of preparation, "skims off" various layers of meaning.

Yuri Lotman

Semiotics of Cinema. Trans. Mark E. Suino. Ann Arbor: Michigan Slavic Contributions. 1976.

The relation between language and experience is often misunderstood. Language is not a more or less systematic inventory of the various items of experience which seem relevant to the individual, as is so often naively assumed, but is also a self-contained, creative symbolic organization, which not only refers to experience largely acquired without its help but actually defines experience for us by reason of its formal completeness and because of our unconscious projection of its implicit expectations into the field of experience.

Edward Sapir

"The Status of Linguistics as a Science." *Language.* 1929.

Such categories as number, gender, case, tense, mode, voice, "aspect" and a host of others, many of which are not recognized...are, of course, derivative of experience at last analysis, but, once abstracted from experience, they are systematically elaborated in language and are not so much discovered in experience as imposed upon it because of the tyrannical hold that linguistic form has upon our orientation in the world.

Edward Sapir

"The Status of Linguistics as a Science." *Language.* 1929.

Codes and subcodes are applied to the message [text] in the light of a general framework of cultural references, which constitutes the receiver's patrimony of knowledge: his ideological, ethical, religious standpoints, his psychological attitudes, his tastes, his value systems, etc.

Umberto Eco

The Role of the Reader: Explorations in the Semiotics of Texts. Bloomington: Indiana University Press. 1984.

There is no such thing as a good or a bad style. It all depends on how the film maker would have us see his narrative. For Eisenstein, a montage-based style was appropriate for *Potemkin;*

an expressionistic style was better for *Ivan the Terrible*. *Potemkin* is concerned with the idea of revolt—the factors that make a society turn on its masters. For that purpose, because it shows contrasts and juxtapositions clearly, montage works well. But for the study of a paranoiac personality, an expressionist style is more appropriate—hence the severe camera angles, long-held shots, and deep shadows of *Ivan*.

Charles Eidsvik
Cineliteracy: Film Among the Arts. New York: Random House. 1978.

This inherently interactive—dialogic—nature of discourse and consciousness (since, as we shall see, consciousness is constituted by language) accounts for the constant generation of new meaning. It also produces a complex understanding of time. Meaning is produced or realized only in the specific utterance of a communication event, that is in a precise historical actualization. However, every utterance is also a responsive link in the continuous chain of other utterances which, in effect, constitute the continuity of human consciousness.

Pam Morris, ed.
The Bakhtin Reader: Selected Writings of Bakhtin, Medvedev, Voloshinov. London: Edward Arnold. 1984.

Between word and image, between what is depicted by language and what is uttered by plastic form, the unity begins to dissolve; a single and identical meaning is not immediately common to them. And if it is true that the image still has the function of speaking, of transmitting something consubstantial with language, we must recognize that it already no longer says the *same thing;* and that by its own plastic values painting engages in an experiment that will take it farther and father from language, whatever the superficial identity of the theme. Figure and speech still illustrate the same fable of folly in the same moral world, but already they take two different directions, indicating

Michel Foucault

it in a still barely perceptible scission, what will be
the great line of cleavage
in the Western experience
of madness.

Michel Foucault

Madness and Civilization: A History of Insanity in the Age of Reason. New York: Vintage Books. 1973.

Freed from wisdom and from the teaching that organized it, the image begins to gravitate about its own madness. Paradoxically, this liberation derives from a proliferation of meaning, from a self-multiplication of significance, weaving relationships so numerous, so intertwined, so rich, that they can no longer be deciphered except in the esoterism of knowledge. Things themselves become so burdened with attributes, signs, allusions that they finally lose their own form. Meaning is no longer read in an immediate perception, the figure no longer speaks for itself; between the knowledge which animates it and the form into which it is transposed, a gap widens. It is free for the dream.

Michel Foucault

Madness and Civilization: A History of Insanity in the Age of Reason. New York: Vintage Books. 1973.

Why traces? And by what right do we reintroduce grammatics at the moment when we seem to have neutralized every substance, be it phonic, graphic, or otherwise?...It is a question, rather, of producing a new concept of writing. This concept can be called *gram* or *différance.* The play of differences suppose, in effect, syntheses and referrals which forbid at any moment, or in any sense, that a simple element be *present* in and of itself, referring only itself. Whether in order of spoken or written discourse, no element can function as a sign without referring to another element which itself is not simply present.

Jacques Derrida

Positions. Trans. Alan Bass. Chicago: The University of Chicago Press. 1981.

Jacques Derrida

There are only, everywhere, differences and traces of traces. The gram, then, is the most general concept of semiology—which thus become grammatology—and it covers not only the field of writing in the restricted sense, but also the field of linguistics. The advantage of this concept—provided that it is surrounded by a certain interpretive context, for no more than any other conceptual element it does not signify, or suffice, by itself—is that in principle it neutralizes the phonologistic propensity of the "sign," and, *in fact counterbalances* it by liberating the entire scientific field of "graphic substance" (history and systems of writing beyond the bounds of the West) whose interest is not minimal, but which so far has been left in the shadows of neglect. The gram as *différance,* then, is a structure and a movement no longer conceivable on the basis of presence/absence.

Jacques Derrida

Positions. Trans. Alan Bass. Chicago: The University of Chicago Press. 1981.

The tendency to interpret everything in an artistic text as meaningful is so great that we rightfully consider nothing as accidental in a work of art.

Yuri Lotman

The Structure of the Artistic Text. Ann Arbor: Michigan Slavic Contributions. 1977.

When we think about those phenomena in which mimicry is likely to play a role, we enumerate such things as dress, mannerisms, facial expressions, speech, stage acting, artistic creation, and so forth, but we never think of desire…. Imitation does not merely draw people together, it pulls them apart. Paradoxically, it can do these two things simultaneously.

Rene Girard

A Theatre of Envy: William Shakespeare. New York: Oxford University Press. 1991.

A logo works on several psychological levels, from the iconic to the mythic. At the iconic level, a symbol such as the V-shaped ears of the Playboy logo simply represents the shape of rabbit ears; but at a mythic level, it taps into the idea of the power of the feminine form and its many archetypal connotations.

Marcel Danesi

X-Rated: The Power of Mythic Symbolism in Popular Culture. New York: Palgrave. 2009.

Contrary to what one might expect, criticism must prevent itself from seeing some sort of object (whether it is the person of the author seen as an Other, or his work considered as a Thing); for what must be arrived at is a subject, which is to say a spiritual activity that one cannot understand except by putting oneself in its place and causing it to play again within us its role as subject.

Georges Poulet

Quoted in R. Scholes. *Structuralism in Literature.* New Haven, NJ: Yale University Press. 1974.

The literary work has two poles, which we might call the artistic and the aesthetic: the artistic refers to the text created by the author and the aesthetic realization accomplished by the reader. From this polarity it follows that the literary work cannot be completely identical with the text, but in fact must lie halfway between the two.

Wolfgang Iser

"The Reading Process: A Phenomenological Approach." In D. Lodge, ed. *Modern criticism and theory: A Reader.* London: Longman. 1988.

Deconstruction is not a dismantling of the structure of the text but a demonstration that it has already dismantled itself.

Hillis Miller

Quoted in M. H. Abrams. "The Deconstructive Angel" in R.C. Davis and R. Schleifer, eds. *Contemporary Literary Criticism: Literary and Cultural Studies.* Second Edition. New York: Longman. 1989.

Identity here becomes a reflection of "lifestyles" that are closely associated with commercial brands and the products they label, as well as with attitudes and behaviors linked to where we shop, how we buy, and what we eat, wear, and consume. These attributes are in turn associated with income, class, and other economic forces that may appear to permit choice but are in fact largely overdetermined by demographics and socio-economics and are beyond the control of individual consumers.... Branded lifestyles are not merely superficial veneers on deeper identities but have to some degree become substitute identities—forms of acquired character that have the potential to go all the way down to the core. They displace traditional ethnic and cultural traits and overwhelm the voluntary aspects of identity we choose for ourselves.

Benjamin Barber

Consumed: How Markets Corrupt Children, Infantalize Adults, and Swallow Citizens Whole. New York: W.W. Norton. 2007.

The French code for cheese is ALIVE. This makes perfect sense when one considers how the French choose and store cheese. They go to a cheese shop and poke and prod the cheeses, smelling them to learn their ages. When they choose one they take it home and store it at room temperature in a cloche.... The American code for cheese is DEAD. Again, this makes sense in context. Americans "kill" their cheese through pasteurization (unpasteurized cheeses are not allowed into this country), select hunks of cheese that have been prewrapped—mummified if you will—in plastic (like body bags), and store it, still wrapped airtight, in a morgue also known as a refrigerator.

Clotaire Rapaille
The Culture Code. New York: Broadway Books. 2006.

It is a common error to believe that value is inherent in the article. Value does not reside in the merchandise, but in the mind of the customer. In other words, it is a mental concept. The function of [marketing] is to create value, to build up in the mind of the reader a high regard for the goods.

Paul Wesley Ivey
Quoted in Kalman Applbaum. *The Marketing Era: From Professional Practice to Global Provisioning.* Routledge: New York. 2004.

For Aristotle and the neo-Aristotelians, everything in a work of art exists for some ultimate purpose, which is the characteristic emotion or peculiar pleasure of the work itself as an object consumed. For the Formalists everything in the work exists in order to permit the work to come into being in the first place.

Fredric Jameson
The prison-house of language: a critical account of structuralism and Russian formalism. Princeton, NJ: Princeton University Press. 1972.

Viktor Shklovsky

The end of art is to give a sensation of the object as seen, not recognized. The technique of art is to make things "unfamiliar," to make forms obscure, so as to increase the difficulty and the duration of perception…. In art, it is our experience of the process of construction that counts, not the final product.

Viktor Shklovsky

"Art as Techniques." In R. C. Davis and R. Schleifer, eds. *Contemporary Literary Criticism: Literary and Cultural Studies*. Second Edition. New York: Longman. 1989.

Every extra-artistic prose discourse—in any of its forms, quotidian, rhetorical, scholarly—cannot fail to be oriented toward the "already uttered," the "already known," the "common opinion" and so forth. The dialogic orientation of discourse is a phenomenon that is, of course, a property of any discourse.

M.M. Bakhtin

The dialogic imagination. Michael Holquist, ed. Trans. Caryl Emerson and Michael Holquist. Austin, TX: University of Texas Press. 1984.

The strength of montage resides in this, that it includes in the creative process the emotions and mind of the spectator. The spectator is compelled to proceed along that selfsame creative road that the author traveled in creating the image. The spectator not only sees the represented elements of the finished work, but also experiences the dynamic process of the emergence and assembly of the image just as it was experienced by the author.

Sergei Eisenstein

Sergei Eisenstein

The Film Sense. New York: Harcourt. 1974.

The notion that linguistics might be useful in studying other cultural phenomena is based on two fundamental insights: first, that social and cultural phenomena are not simply material objects or events but objects and events with meaning, and hence signs; and second, that they do not have essence but are defined by a network of relations.

Jonathan Culler

Ferdinand de Saussure. Revised Edition. Ithaca, NY: Cornell University Press. 1976.

This book has a double theoretical framework: on the one hand, an Ideological critique bearing on the language of so-called mass culture; on the other, a first attempt to analyze semiologically the mechanics of this language. I had just read Saussure and as a result acquired the conviction that by treating "collective representations" as sign-systems, one might hope to go further than the pious show of unmasking them and account in detail for the mystification which transforms petit-bourgeois culture into a universal nature.

Roland Barthes
Mythologies. New York: Hill & Wang. 1972.

Thinking consists not of "happenings in the head" (though happenings there and elsewhere are necessary for it to occur) but of a traffic in what have been called, by G. H. Mead and others—significant symbols—words for the most part but also gestures, drawings, musical sounds, mechanical devices like clocks, or natural objects like jewels—anything, in fact, that is disengaged from its mere actuality and used to impose meaning upon experience. From the point of view of any particular individual, such symbols are largely given. He finds them already current in the community in which is he is born and they remain, with some additions, subtractions, and partial alterations he may or may not have had a hand in, in circulation when he dies.

Clifford Geertz
The Interpretation of Cultures. New York: Basic Books. 1977.

Metaphor is for most people a device of the poetic imagination and the rhetorical flourish—a matter of extraordinary rather than ordinary language. Moreover, metaphor is typically viewed as a characteristic of language alone, a matter of words rather than thought or action. For this reason, most people think they can get along perfectly well without metaphor. We have found, on the contrary, that metaphor is pervasive in everyday life, not just in language but in thought and action. Our ordinary conceptual system, in terms of which we both think and act, is fundamentally metaphoric in nature.

George Lakoff and Mark Johnson
Metaphors We Live By. Chicago: University of Chicago Press. 1980.

The concepts that govern our thought are not just matters of the intellect. They also govern our everyday functioning, down to the most mundane details. Our concepts structure what we perceive, how we get around in the world, and how we relate to other people. Our conceptual system thus plays a central role in defining our everyday realities. If we are right in suggesting that our conceptual system is largely metaphorical, what we experience and what we do every day is very much a matter of metaphor.

George Lakoff and Mark Johnson
Metaphors We Live By. Chicago: University of Chicago Press. 1980.

Metaphor and metonymy are different kinds of processes. Metaphor is principally a way of conceiving of one thing in terms of another, and its primary function is understanding. Metonymy, on the other hand, has primarily a referential function, that is, allows us to use one entity to stand for another. But metonymy is not merely a referential device. It also serves the function of providing understanding.

George Lakoff and Mark Johnson
Metaphors We Live By. Chicago: University of Chicago Press. 1980.

The state of being envied is what constitutes glamour. And publicity is the process of manufacturing glamour.... Publicity is never a celebration of pleasure-in-itself. Publicity is always about the future buyer. It offers him an image of himself made glamorous by the product or opportunity it is trying to sell. The image then makes him envious of himself as he might be. Yet what makes this self-which-he-might-be enviable? The envy of others. Publicity is about social relations, not objects.

John Berger
Ways of Seeing. New York: Penguin. 1972.

What it comes down to is this: Buck teeth imply people are dumb. Large canines imply aggressiveness. Weak chins imply passivity, while strong chins imply a macho, studly personality. I don't know who made these up, but the fact is, they're cultural standards.

Jeffrey Morley

The Wall Street Journal. June 16, 1982.

Digital systems do not use continuously variable representative relationships. Instead, they translate all input into binary structures of 0s and Is, which can then be stored, transferred, or manipulated at the level of numbers or "digits" (so called because etymologically, the word descends from the digits on our hands with which we count out those numbers. Thus a phone call on a digital system will be encoded as a series of these 0s and Is and sent over the wires as binary information to be reinterpreted as speech on the other end.

Peter Lunenfeld, ed.

The Digital Dialectic: New Essays on New Media. Cambridge, MA: M.I.T. Press. 1999.

To be naked is to be oneself. To be nude is to be seen as naked by others and yet not recognized for oneself. A naked body has to be seen as an object in order to become a nude. (The sight of it as an object stimulates the use of it as an object.) Nakedness reveals itself. Nudity is placed on display.

John Berger

Ways of Seeing. New York: Penguin. 1972.

The veil is to clothing what the curtain is to the theater. It simultaneously reveals and conceals, marking a space of transgression and expectation; it leads the spectators to "fantasize about 'the real thing' in anticipation of seeing it." The veil as a sign of the female or the feminine has a long history in Western culture, whether its context is religious chastity (the nun, the bride, the orthodox Muslim woman) or erotic play (the Dance of the Seven Veils). But presuppositions about the gendered function of the veil—that it is worn to mystify, to tantalize, to sacralize, to protect or to put out of bounds—are susceptible to cultural misprision as well as fetishization.

Marjorie Garber

Vested Interests: Cross-Dressing and Cultural Anxiety. New York: Routledge. 1997.

To say that Omo cleans in depth…is to assume that linen is deep, which no one had previously thought, and this unquestionably results in exalting it…. As for foam, it is well-known that is signifies luxury…. Foam can even be the sign of a certain spirituality, inasmuch as the spirit has the reputation of being able to make something out of nothing…. What matters is the art of having disguised the abrasive function of the detergent under the delicious image of a substance at once deep and airy which can govern the molecular order of the material without damaging it.

Roland Barthes

Mythologies. Trans. A. Lavers. New York: Hill & Wang. 1972.

The Middle Ages never forgot that all things would be absurd, if their meaning were exhausted in their function and their place in the phenomenal world, if by their essence they did not reach into a world beyond this. This idea of a deeper significance in ordinary things is familiar to us as well, independently of religious convictions: as an indefinite feeling which may be called up at any moment, by the sound of raindrops on the leaves or by the lamplight on the table…. "When we see all things in God, and refer all things to Him, we read in common matters superior expressions of meaning." (William James: *Varieties of Religious Experience,* p.475)

J. Huizinga

The Waning of the Middle Ages. Garden City, NY: Anchor Books. 1954.

Here, then is the psychological foundation from which symbolism arises. In God nothing is empty of sense.... So the conviction of a transcendental meaning in all things seeks to formulate itself. About the figure of the Divinity a majestic system of correlated figures crystallizes, which all have reference to Him, because all things derive their meaning from Him. The world unfolds itself like a vast whole of symbols, like a cathedral of ideas. It is the most richly rhythmical conception of the world, a polyphonous expression of eternal harmony.

J. Huizinga

The Waning of the Middle Ages. Garden City, NY: Anchor Books. 1954.

From the causal point of view, symbolism appears as a sort of short-circuit of thought. Instead of looking for the relation between two things by following the hidden detours of their causal connections, thought makes a leap and discovers their relation, not in a connection of cause or effects, but in a connection of signification or finality.

J. Huizinga

The Waning of the Middle Ages. Garden City, NY: Anchor Books. 1954.

The fact that French toys literally prefigure the world of adult functions obviously cannot but prepare the child to accept them all, by constituting for him, even before he can think about it, the alibi of a Nature which has at all times created soldiers, postmen and Vespas. Toys here reveal the list of all the things the adult does not find unusual: war, bureaucracy, ugliness, Martians, etc. It is not so much in fact, the imitation which is the sign of an abdication, as its literalness.

Roland Barthes

Mythologies. Trans. A. Lavers. New York: Hill & Wang. 1972.

The role of the other's word was enormous at that time: there were Quotations that were openly and reverently emphasized as such, or that were half-hidden, half-conscious, correct, intentionally distorted, deliberately reinterpreted and so forth.... One of the best authorities on medieval parody...states outright that the history of medieval literature and its Latin literature in particular "is the history of appropriation, reworking and imitation of someone else's property."

M. M. Bakhtin

The Dialogic Imagination: Four Essays. Trans. C. Emerson and M. Holquist. Austin, TX: University of Texas Press. 1981.

A garment, an automobile, a dish of cooked food, a gesture, a film, a piece of music, an advertising image, a piece of furniture, a newspaper headline—these indeed appear to be heterogeneous objects. What might they have in common? This at least: all are signs. When I walk through the streets—or through life—and encounter these objects, I apply to all of them, if need be without realizing it, one and the same activity, which is that of a certain reading: modern man, urban man, spends his time reading. He reads, first of all and above all, images, gestures, behaviors: this car tells me the social status of its owner, this garment tells me quite precisely the degree of its wearer's conformism or eccentricity.

Roland Barthes

The Semiotic Challenge. Berkeley, CA: University of California Press. 1994.

Since it can concentrate a tremendous amount of information into the "area" of a very small text (cf. The length of a short story by Checkov and a psychology textbook) an artistic text manifests yet another feature: it transmits different information to different readers in proportion to each one's comprehension; it provides the reader with a language in which each successive portion of information may be assimilated with repeated reading.

It behaves as a kind of living organism which has a feedback channel to the reader and thereby instructs him.

Yuri Lotman

The Structure of the Artistic Text. Trans. Gail Lenhoff and Ronald Vroon. Ann Arbor, MI: Michigan Slavic Contributions. 1977.

Rawness, we know, is the tutelary divinity of Japanese food: On it everything is dedicated, and if Japanese cooking is always performed in front of the eventual diner (a fundamental feature of this cuisine), this is probably because it is so important to consecrate by spectacle the death of what is being honored.... Japanese rawness is essentially visual: it denotes a certain colored state of the flesh or vegetable substance (it being understood that color is never exhausted by a catalogue of tints, but refers to a whole tactility of substance; thus sashimi exhibits not so much colors as resistances: those which vary the flesh of raw fish causing it to pass, from one end of the tray to the other, through the stations of the soggy, the fibrous, the elastic, the compact, the rough, the slippery).

Roland Barthes

Empire of Signs. Trans. Richard Howard. New York: Hill & Wang. 1982.

The mechanism of myth is the way that habitual representations tangle themselves up in everyday objects and practices so that these ideological meanings come to seem natural, the common-sense reality of that object or practice. There are therefore two systems of meaning: the denotative and the connotative, the "object language" (the film, the toy, the meal, the car inasmuch as they signify) and the myth which attaches itself to it, which takes advantage of the form of this denotative language to insinuate itself.

Rosalind Coward and John Ellis

Language and Materialism: Developments in Semiology and the Theory of the Subject. London: Routledge & Kegan Paul. 1977.

Since the meaning of a sign depends on the code within which it is situated, codes provide a framework within which signs make sense. Indeed, we cannot grant something the status of a sign if it does not function within a code.... The conventions of codes represent a social dimension in semiotics: a code is a set of practices familiar to users of the medium operating within a broad cultural framework.... When studying cultural practices, semioticians treat as signs any objects or actions which have meaning to the members of a cultural group, seeking to identify the rules or conventions of the codes which underlie the production of meaning within that culture.

Daniel Chandler
Semiotics: The Basics. London: Routledge. 2001.

Riegl stated that one type of artistic procedure, which corresponds to a certain way of looking, is based on the scanning of objects according to their outlines. This trajectory Riegl called the optical. The opposite type of vision, which focuses on surfaces and emphasizes the value of the superficies of objects, Riegl called the haptical (from the Greek *habtein*, "to seize, grasp" or *haptikos* "capable of touching.")...The optical eye merely brushes the surface of things. The haptic or tactile eye penetrates in depth, finding pleasure in textile and grain.

Claude Gandelman
Reading Pictures, Viewing Texts. Bloomington: Indiana University Press. 1991.

Structuralists have generally followed Jakobson and taken the binary opposition as a fundamental operation of the human mind basic to the production of meaning.

Jonathan Culler
Structuralist Poetics. Ithaca, NY: Cornell University Press. 1976.

Psychoanalytic Theory

Psychoanalytic theory can be distinguished from psychotherapy, which uses psychoanalytic principles to help people with their psychological problems. Psychoanalytic theory, as elaborated by Freud and developed by countless other psychologists, focuses upon the unconscious, on the relationship that exists between id, ego and superego elements in our psyches, dreams, the Oedipus complex, and other ways in which our minds function and the way these phenomena are found in cultural works.

Since Freud's time, many developments have been made in psychoanalytic thought, and it has evolved considerably since Freud's early formulations. We can also make a distinction between psychoanalytic theory and the application of this theory to literature, the arts and culture in general by scholars working cultural studies. Psychoanalytic theory allows us to obtain insights into all kinds of literature, from fairy tales to classic novels, and other art forms that we would not recognize if we did not have this tool at our disposal.

The British literary critic Simon Lesser wrote in his book *Fiction and the Unconscious* (1957), "The supreme virtue of psychoanalysis, from the point of view of its utility for literary study, is that it has investigated the very aspects of man's nature with which the greatest writers of fiction have been preoccupied:

the emotional, unconscious or only partly comprehended basis of our behavior." He adds that psychoanalytic theories "make it possible to deal with a portion of our response which was not hitherto accessible to criticism." Freud's suggestion that the Oedipus complex may explain the power of Shakespeare's *Hamlet* is an example of the way psychoanalytic theory can be used to deal with texts. Freud wrote about any number of literary works, and for those interested in psychoanalytic theory, it is well worth consulting his writings. Ernest Jones, another psychoanalytic theorist, wrote a book on *Hamlet* that contains many different psychoanalytic interpretations of the play. In addition to great works of literature and art, we can use psychoanalytic theory to analyze modern texts, such as popular songs, television dramas, advertisements, television commercials, films, and comic books.

Freud recognized that many of the concepts found in psychoanalytic theory would seem "absurd" to people. To some degree this is due to the fact that many people who "know" Freud is ridiculous have never read his works. And Freud is continually being declared "dead" and no longer influential, though he is continually being reborn and rediscovered. Ironically, many of Freud's ideas and terms are now part of our everyday thinking and conversation. I offer some selections that deal with developments in psychoanalytic theory since Freud and Jung's days. Psychoanalytic theory, like all theories, keeps evolving.

Psychoanalysis is the name (1) of a procedure for the investigation of mental processes which are almost inaccessible any other way, (2) of a method (based upon that investigation) for the treatment of neurotic disorders and (3) of a collection of psychological information obtained along those lines which is gradually being accumulated into a new scientific discipline.

Sigmund Freud

Character and Culture. Philip Rieff, ed. New York: Collier Books. 1963.

It was a triumph of the interpretative art of psychoanalysis when it succeeded in demonstrating that certain common mental acts of normal people, for which no one had hitherto attempted to put forward a psychological explanation, were to be regarded in the same light as the symptoms of neurotic: that is to say they had a *meaning*, which was unknown to the subject, but which could easily be discovered by analytic means…. A class of material was brought to light which is calculated better than any other to stimulate a belief in the existence of unconscious mental acts even in people to whom the hypothesis of something at once mental and unconscious might seem strange and even absurd.

Sigmund Freud

Character and Culture. Philip Rieff, ed. New York: Collier Books. 1963.

We may say that id comprises the psychic representatives of the drives, the ego consists of those functions which have to do with the individual's relation to his environment, and the superego comprises the moral precepts of our minds as well as our ideal aspirations.

Charles Brenner

An Elementary Textbook of Psychoanalysis. Garden City, NY: Doubleday. 1974.

The female genitalia are symbolically represented by all such objects as share with them the property of enclosing a space or are capable as acting as receptacles: such as pits, hollows and caves, and also jars and bottles, and boxes of all sorts and sizes, chests, coffers, pockets, and so forth. Ships too come into this category. Many symbols refer rather to the uterus than to all the other genital organs: thus cupboards, stoves and above all, rooms. Room symbolism here links up with that of houses, whilst doors and gates represent the genital opening...yet another noteworthy symbol of the female genital organ is a jewel case.

Sigmund Freud
A General Introduction to Psycho-Analysis. New York: Washington Square Press. 1924.

Very little of the way Freud understood and practiced psycho-analysis has remained simply intact. The major pillars of his theorizing—instinctual drives, the centrality of the Oedipus complex, the motivational primacy of sex and aggression—have all been challenged and fundamentally transformed in contemporary psychoanalytic thought. And Freud's basic technical principles—analytic neutrality, the systematic frustration of the patient's wishes, a regression of an infantile neurosis—have likewise been reconceptualized, revised, and transformed by current clinicians.

Stephen A. Mitchell and Margaret J. Black
Freud and Beyond: A History of Modern Psychoanalytic Thought. New York: Basic Books. 1996.

Carl Jung

We do not assume that each new-born animal creates its own instincts as an individual acquisition, and we must not suppose that human individuals invent their specific human ways with every new birth. Like the instincts, the collective thought patterns of the human mind are innate and inherited. They function, when the occasion arises, in more or less the same way in all of us.

Carl Jung
Man and His Symbols. Garden City, NY: Doubleday. 1964.

Blink is concerned with the very smallest components of our everyday lives—the content and origin of those instantaneous impressions and conclusions that spontaneously arise whenever we meet a new person or confront a complex situation or have to make a decision under conditions of stress. When it comes to the task of understanding ourselves and our world, I think we pay too much attention to those grand themes and too little to the particulars of those fleeing moments. But what would happen if we took our instincts seriously? What if we stopped scanning the horizon with our binoculars and began instead examining our own decision making and behavior through the most powerful of microscopes?

Malcolm Gladwell
Blink. The Power of Thinking Without Thinking. New York: Bay Back Books. 2005.

Throughout the inhabited world, in all times and under every circumstance, the myths of man have flourished; and they have been the living inspiration of whatever else may have appeared out of the activities of the human body and mind. It would not be too much to say that myth is the secret opening through which the inexhaustible energies of the cosmos pour into human cultural manifestation. Religions, philosophies, arts, the social forms of primitive and historic man, prime discoveries in science and technology, the very dreams that blister sleep, boil up from the basic, magic ring of myth.

Joseph Campbell
The Hero With A Thousand Faces. New York: MFJ Books. 1949.

The passion of the signifier now becomes a new dimension of the human condition in that it is not only man who speaks, but that in man and through man *it* speaks...that his nature is woven by effects in which is to be found the structure of language, of which he becomes the material, and that therefore there resounds in him, beyond what could be conceived of by a psychology of ideas, the relation of speech.

J. Lacan
Ecrits: A selection. Trans. Alan Sheridan. New York: Norton. 1977.

Lacan was a creature less of psychoanalysis as a clinical discipline and international movement than of French intellectual life. There is no better example than Lacan's work of the way psychoanalysis in different countries takes on a distinctly national character. Lacan's presentations were spectacles, filled with the conceptual and verbal gamesmanship characteristic of the French intelligentsia: sweeping philosophical, political, and literary references and allusions, a contemptuous, combative posturing (the title of Julia Kristeva's novel depicting the intellectual world in which Lacan lived is, tellingly, *The Samurai*), and a complex blend of authoritarian fiat and antiauthoritarian defiance.

Stephen A. Mitchell and Margaret J. Black.
Freud and Beyond: A History of Modern Psychoanalytic Thought. New York: Basic Books. 1996.

For the first five decades in the history of psychoanalytic thought (up until Freud's death in 1939), it would have been tenable to argue that psychoanalysis *was* largely the invention of Freud's singular genius. Freud regarded psychoanalysis as a form of treatment, but also as a new branch of science. He carefully tended his creation and it grew up around him. Those taught and analyzed by Freud were justifiably impressed with his early discoveries; they admired him and let him take the lead. Freud also regarded psychoanalysis as a quasi-political movement, and proved himself a dominant leader, wary of opposition, often regarding others' creativity and originality as signs of disloyalty.

Stephen A. Mitchell and Margaret J. Black

Freud and Beyond: A History of Modern Psychoanalytic Thought. New York: Basic Books. 1996.

On an overt level fairy tales teach little about the specific conditions of life in modern mass society; these tales were created long before it came into being. But more can be learned from them about the inner problems of human beings, and of the right solutions to their predicaments in any society, than from any other type of story within a child's comprehension.

Bruno Bettelheim

The Uses of Enchantment: The Meaning and Importance of Fairy Tales. New York: Knopf. 1976.

Since the child at every moment of his life is exposed to the society in which he lives, he will certainly learn to come with its conditions, provided his inner resources permit him to do so.... Through the centuries (if not millennia) during which, in their retelling, fairy tales became ever more refined, they came to convey at the same time overt and covert meanings—came to speak simultaneously to all levels of the human personality, communicating in a manner which reaches the uneducated mind of the child as well as that of the sophisticated adult.

Bruno Bettelheim

The Uses of Enchantment: The Meaning and Importance of Fairy Tales. New York: Knopf. 1976.

The most celebrated and influential modern doctrines, those of Marx and Freud, actually amount to an elaborate system of hermeneutics, aggressive and imperious theories of interpretation.... For Marx, social events like revolutions and wars; for Freud, the events of individual lives (like neurotic symptoms and slips of the tongue) as well as texts (like a dream or a work of art)—are all treated as occasions for interpretation. According to Marx and Freud, these events only *seem* to be intelligible. Actually, they have no meaning without interpretation. To understand is to interpret. And to interpret is to restate the phenomenon, in effect to find an equivalent for it...interpretation is the revenge of the intellect upon art. Even more. It is the revenge of the intellect upon the world.

Susan Sontag

Against Interpretation. New York: Laurel Books. 1969.

Robinson Crusoe is related to three essential themes of modern civilization—which we can briefly designate as "Back to Nature," "The Dignity of Labor," and "Economic Man." Robinson Crusoe seems to have become a kind of culture hero representing all three of these related but not wholly congruent ideas. It is true that if we examine what Defoe actually wrote and what he may be thought to have intended, it appears that *Robinson Crusoe* hardly supports some of the symbolic uses to which the pressure of the needs of our society has made it serve. But this, of course, is in keeping with the status of *Robinson Crusoe* as a myth, for we learn as much from the varied shapes that a myth takes in men's minds as from the form in which it first arose. It is not an author but a society that metamorphoses a story into a myth, by retaining only what its unconscious needs dictate and forgetting everything else.

Ian Watt

"Robinson Crusoe as Myth." From *Essays in Criticism: A Quarterly Journal of Literary Criticism*, April 1951. Reprinted in Robert N. Wilson, ed. *The Arts in Society.* Upper Saddle River, NJ: Prentice-Hall. 1964.

A joke is a play upon form. It brings into relation disparate elements in such a way that one accepted pattern is challenged by the appearance of another which in some way was hidden in the first. I confess that I find Freud's definition of the joke highly satisfactory. The joke is an image of the relaxation of conscious control in favor of the subconscious.... The joke merely affords opportunity for realizing that an accepted pattern has no necessity. Its excitement lies in the suggestion that any particular ordering of experience may be arbitrary and subjective. It is frivolous in that it produces no real alternative, only an exhilarating sense of freedom from form in general.

Mary Douglas

Implicit Meanings: Essays in Anthropology. London: Routledge and Kegan Paul. 1975.

Our conceptions always arise through comparison. "Were it always light we should not distinguish between light and dark, and accordingly could not have either the conception of, nor the word for, light...." "It is clear that everything on this planet is relative and has independent existence only in so far as it is distinguished in its relations to and from other things."

Sigmund Freud

"The Antithetical Sense of Primal Words." A Review of a Pamphlet by Karl Abel. *Uber den Gegensinn der Urworte, 1884*. In S. Freud, *Character and Culture*. Philip Rieff, ed. New York: Collier Books. 1963.

Rock is made *in order to* have emotional, social, physical, commercial results; it is not music made "for its own sake."...Rock is, in a sense, primitive. It uses a primitive understanding of how sounds and rhythms—prelinguistic devices—have their emotional and physical effects. Its sound effects are those of daily life. The sound questions raised are nonmusical: Why do we respond the way we do to a baby's cry, a stranger's laugh, a loud, steady beat? Because so much of rock music depends on the social effects of the voice, the questions about how rock's effects are produced are vocal not musical. What makes a voice haunting? sexy? chilling?

Simon Frith

Sound Effects: Youth, Leisure, and the Politics of Rock'n'Roll. New York: Pantheon. 1981.

Applying the psychoanalytic model of the human personality, fairy tales carry important messages to the conscious, preconscious, and the unconscious mind, on whatever level each is functioning at the time. By dealing with universal human problems, particularly those which occupy the child's mind, these stories speak to his budding ego and encourage its development, while at the same time relieving preconscious and unconscious pressures. As the stories unfold, they give conscious credence and body to id pressures and show ways to satisfy these that are in line with ego and superego requirements.

Bruno Bettelheim

The Uses of Enchantment: The Meaning and Importance of Fairy Tales. New York: Knopf. 1976.

Being entirely honest with oneself is a good exercise. Only one idea of general value has occurred to me. I have found love of the mother and jealousy of the father in my own case too, and now believe it to be a general phenomenon of early childhood, even if it does not always occur so early in children who have been made hysterics....If that is the case, the gripping power of *Oedipus Rex*, in spite all rational objections to the inexorable fate that the story presupposes becomes intelligible, and one can understand why later fate dramas were such failures. Our feelings rise against any arbitrary individual fate...but the Greek myth seizes on a compulsion which everyone recognizes because he has felt traces of it himself. Every member of the audience was once a budding Oedipus in fantasy, and this dream-fulfillment played out in reality causes everyone to recoil in horror, with the full measure of repression which separates his infantile from his present state.

The idea has passed through my head that the same thing may lie at the root of *Hamlet*. I am not thinking of Shakespeare's conscious intentions, but supposing rather that he was impelled to write it by a real event because his unconscious

Sigmund Freud

understood that of his hero. How can one explain the hysteric Hamlet's phrase "So conscience doth make cowards of us all," and his hesitation to avenge his father by killing his uncle, when he himself so casually sends his courtiers to their death and dispatches Laertes to quickly? How better than by the torment roused in him by the obscure memory that he himself had meditated the same deed against his father because of passion for his mother—"use every man after his desert and who should scape whipping?"

Sigmund Freud

Letter to Wilhelm Fliess. Oct. 15, 1897. Quoted in Martin Grotjahn. *Beyond Laughter: Humor and the Subconscious.* New York: McGraw-Hill. 1966.

Real-world vision is intimately connected with emotion, which, in turn, is tied to our functional needs as biological and social creatures. When we look at the world, we are strongly predisposed to attend to certain kinds of objects or situations and to react in certain kinds of ways. These predispositions reflect the influence of culture, but...they have also been shaped to a certain degree by biological evolution. In short, real-world vision comes with a set of built-in response tendencies. Consequently, to the extent that a picture can reproduce the significant visual

features of real-world experiences, it may also be able to exploit
the response tendencies that are associated with those features.

Paul Messaris

Visual Persuasion: The Role of Images in Advertising. Thousand Oaks, CA:
Sage. 1997.

In *Hamlet*, the very absence of a case against revenge becomes a
powerful intimation of what the modern world is really about.
Even at those later stages in our culture when physical revenge
and blood feuds completely disappeared or were limited to
such marginal milieu as the underworld, it would seem that no
revenge play, not even a play of reluctant revenge, could strike a
really deep chord in the modern psyche. In reality the question
is never entirely settled, and the strange void at the center of
Hamlet becomes a symbolic expression of the Western and modern malaise, no less powerful than the most brilliant attempts to
define the problem, such as Dostoyevski's underground revenge.

René Girard

A Theater of Envy: William Shakespeare. New York: Oxford University
Press. 1991.

If an unlimited imagination as to what one might become is the
heritage of the play age, then the adolescent's willingness to put
his trust in those peers and leading, or misleading, elders who
will give imaginative, if not illusory, scope to his aspirations is
only too obvious. By the same token, he objects violently to all
"pedantic" limitations of self-images and will be ready to settle
by loud accusation all his guiltiness over the excessiveness of his
ambition.

Erik H. Erikson

Identity, Youth, and Crisis. New York: W.W. Norton. 1968.

The changes in values and behavior, the increased passivity and
the lack of wholehearted and lasting commitments among the
young (and not so young), are undoubtedly due to numerous

factors among which television has not been established as the essential one. However, we cannot remain complacent and let things drift along until demonstratable, permanent, serious side effects are undermining the health of the population.

J. E. Heuscher

A Psychiatric Study of Myths and Fairy Tales. Springfield, IL: Charles C. Thomas. 1963.

The text as such offers different "schematized views" through which the subject matter of the work can come to light, but the actual bringing to light is an action of *Konkretisation.* If this is so, then the literary work has two poles, which we might call the artistic, and the aesthetic: the artistic refers to the text created by the author, and the aesthetic to the realization accomplished by the reader. From this polarity it follows that the literary work cannot be completely identical with the text, or with the realization of the text, but in fact must lie halfway between the two. The work is more than the text, for the text only takes on life when it is realized and furthermore the realization is by no means independent of the individual disposition of the reader—though this in turn is acted upon by the different patterns of the text.

Wolfgang Iser

"The Reading Process: A Phenomenological Approach." In David Lodge, ed. *Modern Criticism and Theory: A Reader.* New York: Longman. 1988.

1. To be amused.
2. To see authority figures exalted or deflated.
3. To experience the beautiful.
4. To have shared experiences with others.
5. To satisfy curiosity and be informed.
6. To identify with the deity and the divine plan.
7. To find distraction and diversion.
8. To experience empathy.
9. To experience, in a guilt-free situation, extreme emotions.
10. To find models to imitate.

11. To gain an identity.
12. To gain information about the world.
13. To reinforce our belief in justice.
14. To believe in romantic love.
15. To believe in magic, the marvelous and the miraculous.
16. To see others make mistakes.
17. To see order imposed upon the world.
18. To participate in history (vicariously).
19. To be purged of unpleasant emotions.
20. To obtain outlets for our sexual drives in a guilt-free context.
21. To explore taboo subjects with impunity.
22. To experience the ugly.
23. To affirm moral, spiritual, and cultural values.
24. To see villains in action.

Arthur Asa Berger

Media Analysis Techniques. Third Edition. Thousand Oaks, CA: Sage Publications. 2005.

Group Psychology is therefore concerned with the individual man as a member of a race, of a nation, of a caste, of a profession, of an institution, or as a component part of a crowd of people who have been organized into a group at some particular time for some particular purpose.

Sigmund Freud

Group Psychology and the Analysis of the Ego. In John Rickman, ed. *A General Selection from the Works of Sigmund Freud.* Garden City, NY: Anchor. 1957.

The contrast between Individual Psychology and Social or Group Psychology, which at first glance may seem to be full of significance, loses a great deal of its sharpness when it is examined more closely. It is true that Individual Psychology is concerned with the individual man and explores the paths by which he seeks to find satisfaction for his instincts; but only rarely and under certain exceptional conditions is Individual Psychology in a position to disregard the relations of this individual to others. In the individual's mental life someone else is invariably involved as a model, as an object, as a helper, as an opponent, and so from the very first Individual Psychology is at the same time Social Psychology as well.

Sigmund Freud
Group Psychology and the Analysis of the Ego. In John Rickman, ed. *A General Selection from the Works of Sigmund Freud.* Garden City, NY: Anchor. 1957.

The desire for money is the permanent disposition that the mind displays in an established money economy. Accordingly, the psychologist simply cannot ignore the frequent lament that money is the God of our times…. The feelings stimulated by money have a psychological similarity to this in their own arena. By increasingly becoming the absolutely sufficient expression and equivalent of all values, it rises in a very abstract elevation over the whole broad variety of objects; it becomes the centre in which the most opposing, alien and distant things find what they have in common and touch each other.

Georg Simmel
"Money in Modern Culture." *Theory, Culture & Society.* Vol. 8, no. 3, 1991.

He may find himself on one of two sides. He may discover that he agrees with the prevailing (or winning) view, which boosts his self-confidence and enables him to express himself with an untroubled mind and without any danger of isolation, in conversation, by cutting those who hold different views. Or he may find that the views he holds are losing ground; the more this appears to be so, the more uncertain he will become of himself, and the less he will be inclined to express his opinion.

Elizabeth Noelle-Neumann
"The Spiral of Silence: A Theory of Public Opinion." *Journal of Communication.* Spring, 1974.

The first thing that becomes clear to anyone who compares the dream content with the dream thought is that a work of *condensation* on a large scale has been carried out. Dreams are brief, meagre and laconic in comparison with the range and wealth of dream thoughts. If a dream is written out it may perhaps fill half a page. The analysis setting out the dream thoughts underlying it may occupy six, eight or a dozen times as much space.

Sigmund Freud

The Interpretation of Dreams. New York: Avon. 1900.

The knowledge of the soul of things is possibly a very direct and new and revolutionary way of discovering the soul of man. The power of various types of objects to bring out into the open new aspects of the personality of modern man is great. The more intimate knowledge of as many different types of products a man has, the richer his life will be.... In the final analysis objects motivate our life probably at least as much as the Oedipus complex or childhood experiences do.

Ernest Dichter

The Strategy of Desire. New Brunswick, NJ: Transaction Publications. 2002.

In psychiatry, the love object of the person who suffers from the perversion called fetishism—usually a part of the body or some object belonging to or associated with the love object. The fetish replaces and substitutes for the love object, and although sexual activity with the love object may occur, gratification is possible only if the fetish is present or at least fantasized during such activity. Typical also is the ability of the fetishist to obtain gratification from the fetish alone, in the absence of the love object.

Leland E. Hinsie and Robert Jean Campbell

The Psychiatric Dictionary. Fourth Edition. New York: Oxford University Press. 1970.

Feminist Theory

Feminist thought is an increasingly important component of cultural studies. A number of theorists have written important books that offer a Feminist perspective on mass media, philosophy and other aspects of culture, especially involving the matter of gender and topics related to gender identity. Not all of these theorists are women, I should add. For example, many male writers, such as Goffman and McLuhan, have had interesting things to say about the way women are portrayed in the media. But it is thinkers such as Judith Butler, Helene Cixous, Julia Kristeva, Marjorie Garber, Susan Sontag, bell hooks, Germain Greer, Simone de Beauvoir, and Janice Radway who have offered some of the more compelling arguments about gender and its relation to various aspects of contemporary culture and society.

The first wave of feminism can be said to have begun at the end of the eighteenth century with the writings of Mary Wollstonecraft Godwin, author of *A Vindication of the Rights of Women*, published in 1792. It also developed in the later decades of the nineteenth century in Britain and the United States. A so-called "third wave" of feminism started developing, as a social and political movement, in the sixties and seventies, though it has roots in early feminist thought and actions as early as the 1850s, when it principally focused on gaining equal rights for women. It must be remembered that women originally didn't have the right to vote in the United States. In recent decades, what is sometimes described as "radical" feminism has developed in the sixties, focusing upon the importance of gender and women's search for identity. Many feminists argue that gender is socially constructed which means that our attitudes towards gender and sexuality are not natural but historical. As Amdermahr, Lovell and Wolowitz write in *A Glossary of Feminist Theory* (1977) "the whole gender order in which people, things and behaviour are classified in terms of the distinction between masculine and feminine are socially constructed and has no basis in natural differences between the sexes."

One question feminists face involves how they define women. Are all women the same—regardless or race, ethnicity, socioeconomic class, and cultural differences—because they are all oppressed, or are there important differences among women that have to be considered by Feminist thinkers. Feminist thinking has been influenced by semiotics theory, psychoanalytic theory (Freud asked "What do women want?"), Marxist theory and many other theories. What you find when you read many Feminist thinkers, is that their arguments go far beyond such things as women's political weakness and oppression and involve topics such as the way women are represented in the media and the kind of binary thinking that sees the world in terms of two opposite sexes—one with a penis and one without, one that can bear children and one that can't.

The fact that it is a woman who is seen as cause of the excess and deficiency in the play and again a woman who symbolizes its aesthetic failure begins to look like a repetition. First, of the play itself—Hamlet and his dead father united in the reproach they make of Gertrude for her sexual failing.... Secondly, a repetition of a more fundamental drama of psychic experience as described by Freud, the drama of sexual difference in which the woman is seen as the cause of just such a failure in representation, as something deficient, lacking or threatening to the system and identities which are the precondition not only of integrated aesthetic form but also of so-called normal adult psychic and sexual life.

Jacqueline Rose
"Hamlet—The Mona Lisa of Literature." *Critical Quarterly.* 28,1-2. 1986.

In *God Is My Copilot,* the G.I.'s agreed that what they were fighting for was, after all, the American girl. To us, they said, she meant cokes, hamburgers, and clean places to sleep. Now, the American girl as portrayed by the coke ads has always been an archetype. No matter how much thigh she may be demurely sporting, she is sweet, nonsexual, and immaturely innocent.... Margaret Mead's observations in *Male and Female* are especially relevant to understanding the success of coke ads. It is, she suggests, a result of our child-feeding habits that "Mouths are not a way of being with someone, but rather a way of meeting an impersonal environment. Mother is there to put things—bottles, spoons, crackers, teethers—into your mouth." And so, she adds, the American G.I. abroad puzzled foreigners by endless insistence of having something in his mouth most of the time. Gum, candy, cokes.... The coke has become a kind of rabbit's foot, as it were, for the foreigner. And *Time's* cover (May 15, 1950) pictures the globe sucking a coke. Love that coke, love that American way of life.

Marshall McLuhan
The Mechanical Bride: Folklore of Industrial Man. Boston: Beacon Press. 1951/1967.

Recent psychoanalytic theory hypothesizes that all conventional language and pictorial representation is male-based, for reasons rooted in the psychology of infantile sexuality.... If even everyday viewing is organized along these lines, with patriarchal power relations being reproduced in every depiction of women on a magazine page or billboard, then we are all ideological captives.

Jane Gaines

"Women and representation: Can we enjoy alternative pleasure?" In D. Lazere, ed. *American Media and Mass Culture*. Berkeley, CA: University of California Press. 1987.

A genre is never defined solely by its constitutive set of functions but by interaction between characters and by their development as individuals. As a result, I have assumed further that the romantic genre is additionally defined for the women by a set of characters whose personalities and behaviors can be "coded" or summarized through the course of the reading process in specific ways.… By pursuing similarities in the behaviors of these characters and by attempting to understand what those behaviors signify to these readers, I have sought to avoid summarizing them according to my own beliefs about and standards for gender behavior.

Janet Radway

Reading the Romance: Women, Patriarchy and Popular Literature. Chapel Hill: University of North Carolina Press. 1991.

By women as a category of analysis, I am referring to the crucial assumption that all of us of the same gender, across classes and cultures, are somehow socially constituted as a homogenous group identified prior to the process of analysis. This is an assumption which characterizes much feminist discourse. The homogeneity of women as a group is produced not on the basis of biological essentials but rather on the basis of secondary sociological and anthropological universals. Thus, for instance, in any given piece of feminist analysis, women are characterized as a singular group on the basis of shared oppression.

Chandra Talpade Mohanty

Third World Women and the Politics of Feminism. Bloomington: Indiana University Press. 1991.

Jacques Lacan

Paradoxical as this formulation might seem, it is in order to be the phallus, that is, the signifier of the desire of the Other, that the woman will reject an essential part of her femininity, notably all its attributes through masquerade. It is for what she is not that she expects to be desired and loved. But she finds the signifier of her own desire in the body of the one to whom she addresses her desire for love.

Jacques Lacan

"The Meaning of the Phallus." In Juliet Mitchell and Jacqueline Rose, eds. *Feminine Sexuality: Jacques Lacan and the École Freudienne.* New York: Norton. 1985.

If we can learn, then, to look at the ways in which various groups appropriate and use the mass-produced art of our culture, I suspect we may well begin to understand that although the ideological power of contemporary cultural forms is enormous, indeed sometimes even frightening, that power is not yet all-pervasive, totally vigilant, or complete. Interstices still exist with the social fabric where opposition is carried on by people who are not satisfied by their place within it or by the restricted material and emotional rewards that accompany it.

Janet Radway

Reading the Romance: Women, Patriarchy and Popular Literature. Chapel Hill: University of North Carolina Press. 1991.

Feminist philosophy challenges the entire Western tradition (and not only that tradition). While claiming to be universal and all-inclusive, philosophy has not even included or taken into account, of the woman next door. It certainly has not asked whether she sees things differently, or whether she would ask the same questions in the same way as male philosophers. Thus one of the most radical changes that feminism has provoked in contemporary philosophy is the centrality of the notion of a personal "standpoint"—what Nietzsche called a "perspective." Different people, in different positions, might "see" the world very differently. Thus, a plurality of perspectives might replace the competing demands for a singular "objectivity."

Robert C. Solomon and Kathleen M. Higgins
A Passion for Wisdom: A Very Brief History of Philosophy. New York: Oxford University Press. 1997.

As the car is the symbol of masculinity, so is the house a symbol of femininity. To a woman, her home is like another, larger body and all her mysterious impulses find expression within its walls. Her deepest self is implicated in the texture of the draperies, the casual shape of chairs and tables, the dimensions of a bed. As she trudges from shop to shop—examining, comparing, pondering over this article or that—her choices are determined by an unconscious image of what she is, or dreads to be…. The unconscious fear of "exposing" not their taste alone but their inmost selves is what drives a large number of women into the arms of professional decorators. By leaving decisions to the experts, they disengage themselves from the entire project. Or try to.

Milton R. Saperstein, M.D.
Paradoxes of Everyday Life. New York: Premier Books. 1955.

In philosophy, woman is always on the side of passivity. Every time the question comes up; when we examine kinship structures; whenever a family model is brought into play; in fact as the ontological question is raised; as soon as you ask yourself what is meant by the question "What is it?"; as soon as there is a will to say something. A will: desire, authority—you examine that, and you are led right back—to the father. You can even fail to notice that there's no place at all for women in the operation! In the extreme, the world of "being" can function to the exclusion of the mother—provided there is something of the maternal: and it is the father then who acts—is—the mother. Either the woman is passive; or she doesn't exist. What is left is unthinkable, unthought of. She does not enter into the oppositions, she is not coupled with the father (who is coupled with the son).

Hélène Cixous
"Sorties." In David Lodge, ed. *Modern Criticism and Theory: A Reader.* London: Longman. 1988.

Goffman showed us how women in relation to men have been depicted in inferior and/or child-like positions.... Goffman knew and warned us that advertisements are not reality. Nevertheless, he suggested that ads told us something about real life. The presentation of self to a certain extent is always the presentation of gender. This representation can be reduced merely to the use of power, but the implication could also be more subtle. For example, even in organizations where men and women are used to working together, certain power struggles, even when fought out in the presence of female colleagues, specifically belong to male cultures, like the telling of crude jokes or heavy teasing before the start of actual negotiations. Participation in this kind of impression management is taboo for the women

Lieteke van Vucht Tijssen
"Women Between Modernity and Postmodernity." In Bryan S. Turner, ed. *Theories of Modernity and Postmodernity.* London: Sage Publications. 1991.

Linguistic and textual theories of women's writing ask whether men and women use language differently; whether sex differences in language use can be theorized in terms of biology, socialization, or culture; whether women can create new languages of their own; and whether speaking, reading, and writing are all gender marked.

Elaine Showalter

"Feminist Criticism in the Wilderness." Elaine Showalter, ed. *The New Feminist Criticism.* New York: Pantheon. 1985.

How to deal, for example, with men who show their power by leaning backwards in a chair with their thumbs in their armpit? What should women do if they want or have to portray similar shows of power? And what could be the female equivalent to crude joking or heavy teasing? Thus, women entering a masculine world both suffer from, and cause something of, a culture shock. Although it is less obvious, this discomfort also can be experienced by men when they enter the world of women. When approaching gender differences from this point of view, emancipation means getting to know the other's culture as well as learning how to transgress its borders in a civilized way. Emancipation means communication; it does not necessarily mean identification.

Lieteke van Vucht Tijssen

"Women Between Modernity and Postmodernity." In Bryan S. Turner, ed. *Theories of Modernity and Postmodernity.* London: Sage Publications. 1991.

If it is not possible to say of a *woman* what she is (without running the risk of abolishing her difference), would it perhaps be different concerning the *mother*, since that is the only function of the "other sex" to which we can definitely attribute existence?

Julia Kristeva

"Stabat Mater." In Toril Moi, ed. *The Kristeva Reader.* New York: Columbia University Press. 1986.

Precisely because "female" no longer appears to be a stable notion, its meaning is as troubled and unfixed as "woman," and because both terms gain their troubled significations only as relational terms, this inquiry takes as its focus gender and their relational analysis it suggests. Further, it is no longer clear that feminist theory ought to try to settle the questions of primary identity in order to get on with the task of politics. Instead, we ought to ask, what political possibilities are the consequence of a radical critique of the categories of identity. What new shape of politics emerges when identity as a common ground no longer constrains the discourse on feminist politics?

Judith Butler

General Trouble: Feminism and the Subversion of Identity.
New York: Routledge. 1999.

In Lacan, as in Irigaray's post-Lacanian reformulation of Freud, sexual difference is not a simple binary that retains the metaphysics of substance as its foundation. The masculine "subject" is a fictive construction produced by the law that prohibits incest and forces an infinite displacement of a heterosexualizing desire. The feminine is never a mark of the subject; the feminine is the signification of lack, signified by the Symbolic, a set of differentiating linguistic rules that effectively create sexual difference.

Judith Butler

Judith Butler

General Trouble: Feminism and the Subversion of Identity. New York: Routledge. 1999.

Hysteria is the woman's simultaneous acceptance and refusal of the organization of sexuality under patriarchal capitalism. It is simultaneously what a woman can do both to be feminine and to refuse femininity, within patriarchal discourse. And I think that is exactly what the novel is; I do not believe there is such a thing as female writing, a "woman's voice." There is the hysteric's voice which is *the woman's masculine language* (one has to speak "masculinely" in a phallocentric world) talking about feminine experience. It is both simultaneously the woman novelist's refusal of the woman's world—she is, after all, a novelist—and her construction from within a masculine world of that woman's world.

Juliet Mitchell
Lodge, ed. *Modern Criticism and Theory: A Reader.* London: Longman. 1988.

Three facets of a radical feminist critique that I consider pertinent to communications processes include: the social construction of knowledge and information, especially those assumptions concerning gender; the role of language in supporting gender-based inequalities; and conceptions of "difference" as they challenge masculinist philosophers' assertions about the universality of the human condition and related methodological and political positions.

Kathyryn Cirksena
"Politics and difference: Radical feminist epistemological premises for communication study." *Journal of Communication Inquiry.* 1987.

In her contribution to *Beyond Equality and Difference*, Rose Braidotti (1992) rejects the defence of theoretical reason, the unity of the subject and even of equality (equal to whom, she asks?) as "domination," enlightenment concepts, which have been part of an apparatus of regulation and subordination hidden under the great achievements of rationality and knowledge. This marks her out immediately as a postmodern feminist. The question that has to be asked, she suggests, is that of how we think, what is it to think?

Angel McRobbie
Postmodernism and Popular Culture. London: Routledge. 1985.

Sociological Theory

Sociology is the study of groups and institutions and the role they play in various aspects of our societies. My focus in this section of the book is on theorists whose work has the greatest application to cultural criticism. You will see that sociological theory is extremely diverse in nature and covers many different topics. The classical sociologists of the nineteenth century were interested in everything from suicide to the role of Calvinism in capitalism, from how people relate to one another to the roles social institutions play in our everyday lives.

When I was teaching, my students often became fascinated by the "chicken and egg" problem relating to individuals and society. Does society "create" individuals, which means society is primary, or do individuals, grouped together, form society, which means individuals are primary. For the sociologists, this problem remains an enigma, though you will see I have quotations from some thinkers who argue, pretty persuasively I believe, that society is primary.

I have selected material from some of the greatest sociological thinkers of the twentieth century, such as Max Weber, Georg Simmel and Emile Durkheim. I've also added material by more recent theorists, whose ideas and concepts play an important role in contemporary thinking about social institutions and the relationship that exists between sociological theories and cultural studies, with particular attention to the development of modern consumer cultures. I have written a Sherlock Holmes mystery, *Durkheim is Dead,* about sociological theory, in which Emile Durkheim, Max Weber, Sigmund Freud, and Vladimir Lenin play important roles.

For human beings, society is a primary reality, not just the sum of individual activities, not the contingent manifestations of Mind; and if one wishes to study human behavior, one must grant that there is a social reality. People live not simply among objects and actions but among objects and actions that have meaning, and these meanings cannot be treated as a sum of subjecting perceptions.... In short, sociology, linguistics, and psychoanalytic psychology are possible only when one takes meanings which are attached to and which differentiate objects and actions in society as a primary reality, as facts to be explained. And since meanings are a social product, explanation must be carried out in social terms.

Jonathan Culler

Ferdinand de Saussure. Revised Edition. Ithaca, NY: Cornell University Press. 1986.

It is not true...that human activity can be released from all restraint. Nothing in the world can enjoy such a privilege. All existence being a part of the universe is relative to the remainder; its nature and method of manifestation accordingly depend not only on itself but on other beings, who consequently restrain and regulate it. Here there are only differences of degree and form between the mineral realm and the thinking person. Man's characteristic privilege is that the bond he accepts is not physical but moral; that is, social. He is governed not by a material environment brutally imposed on him, but by a conscience superior to his own, the superiority of which he feels. Because the greater part of his existence transcends the body, he escapes the body's yoke, but is subject to that of society.

Emile Durkheim

Suicide: A Study in Sociology. Trans. J.A. Spaulding and G. Simpson. New York: Free Press. 1952.

What matters to people is how they should live with other people. The great questions of social life are "Who am I?" (To what kind of a group do I belong?) and "What should I do?" (Are there many or few prescriptions I am expected to obey?). Groups are strong or weak according to whether they have boundaries separating them from others. Decisions are taken either for the group as a whole (strong boundaries) or for individuals or families (weak boundaries). Prescriptions are few or many indicating the individual internalizes a large or a small number of behavioral norms to which he or she is bound. By combining boundaries with prescriptions…the most general answers to the questions of social life can be combined to form four different political cultures.

Aaron Wildavsky

"Conditions for a Pluralist Democracy or Cultural Pluralism means More Than One Political Culture in a Country." Unpublished manuscript. 1982.

The variability of an individual's involvement in social life can be adequately captured by two dimensions of sociality: group and grid. *Group* refers to the extent to which an individual is incorporated into bounded units. The greater the incorporation, the more individual choice is subject to group determination. *Grid* denotes the degree to which an individual's life is circumscribed by externally imposed prescriptions. The more binding and extensive the scope of the prescriptions, the less of life that is open to individual negotiation.

Michael Thompson, Richard Ellis, and Aaron Wildavsky

Cultural Theory. Boulder, CO: Westview. 1990.

Georg Simmel

The fact that someone is poor does not mean that he belongs to the specific social category of the "poor."...It is only from the moment that [the poor] are assisted...that they become part of a group characterized by poverty. The group does not remain united by interaction among its members, but by the collective attitude which society as a whole adopts toward it.... Poverty cannot be defined in itself as a quantitative state, but only in terms of the social reaction resulting from a specific situation.... Poverty is a unique sociological phenomenon: a number of individuals who, out of a purely individual fate, occupy a specific organic position within the whole; but this position is not determined by this fate and condition, but rather by the fact that others...attempt to correct this condition.

Georg Simmel
"The Poor." Trans. Claire Jacobson. In *Social Problems, XIII, 2.* Fall 1965.

I shall argue that forms of socialization orient the child towards speech codes which control access to relatively context-tied or relatively context-independent meanings. Thus I shall argue that elaborated codes orient their users towards universalistic meanings. Whereas restricted codes orient, sensitize, their users to particularistic meanings: that the linguistic-realization of the two orders are different, and so are the social relationships which realize them. Elaborated codes are less tied to a given or local structure and thus contain the potentiality of change in principles.

Basil Bernstein

"Social Class, Language and Socialization." In Pier Paolo Giglioli, ed. *Language and social context*. Harmondsworth, England: Penguin. 1972.

Collective representations are the result of an immense co-operation, which stretches out not only into space but into time as well: to make them, a multitude of minds have associated, united, and combined their ideas and sentiments; for them, long generations have accumulated their experience and their knowledge. A special intellectual activity is therefore concentrated in them which is infinitely richer and complexer than that of the individual.

Emile Durkheim

The Elementary Forms of Religious Life. New York: Free Press. 1967.

According to the well-known formula, man is double. There are two beings in him: an individual being which has its foundation in the organism and the circle of whose activities is therefore strictly limited, and a social being, which represents the highest reality in the intellectual and moral order that we can know by observation—I mean society. This duality of our nature has as its consequence in the practical order, the irreducibility of reason to individual experience. In so far as he belongs to society, the individual transcends himself, both when he thinks and when he acts.

Emile Durkheim

The Elementary Forms of Religious Life. New York: Free Press. 1967.

Inasmuch as adornment usually is also an object of considerable value, it is a synthesis of the individual's having and being: it thus transforms mere possession into the sensuous and emphatic perceivability of the individual himself. This is not true of ordinary dress which, neither in respect of having nor being, strikes one as an individual particularity; only the fancy dress, and above all, jewels, which gather the personality's value and significance or radiation as if in a focal point, allow the mere *having* of the person to become a visible quality of its *being*. And this is so, not *although* adornment is something "superfluous," but precisely *because* it is.

Georg Simmel

"Adornment." In Kurt H. Wolff, trans. and ed. *The Sociology of Georg Simmel*. Glencoe: Free Press. 1950.

But when society is disturbed by some painful crisis or by beneficent but abrupt transitions, it is momentarily incapable of exercising this influence; thence come the sudden rises in the curve of suicide.... Appetites, not being controlled by a public opinion, become disoriented, no longer recognize the limits proper to them.... At the very moment when traditional rules have lost their authority, the richer prize offered these appetites stimulates them and makes them more exigent and impatient of control. The state of de-regulation or anomie is thus further heightened by passions being less disciplined, precisely when they need more disciplining.

Emile Durkheim

Suicide: A Study in Sociology. Trans. J.A Spaulding and G. Simpson. New York: Free Press. 1952.

Society is not all the illogical or a-logical, incoherent and fantastic being which has too often been considered. Quite on the contrary, the collective consciousness is the highest form of psychic life, since it is the consciousness of consciousnesses. Being placed outside of and above individual and local contingencies, it sees things only in their permanent and essential aspects, which it crystallizes into communicable ideas. At the same time that it sees from above, it sees farther; at every moment of time it embraces all known reality; that is why it alone can furnish the minds with the moulds which are applicable to the totality of things and which make it possible to think of them.

Emile Durkheim

Moral Education: A Study in the Theory and Application of Sociology to Education. New York: The Free Press. 1973.

The scientific treatment of value judgments may not only understand and empathically analyze the desired ends and the ideals which underline them; it can also "judge" them critically. This criticism can…be not more than a formal logical judgment of historically given value judgments and ideas, a testing of the ideals according to the postulate of the internal *consistency* of the desired end…. It can assist [the acting person] in become aware of the ultimate standards of value which he does not make explicit to himself, or which he must presuppose in order to be logical…. As to whether the person expressing these value judgments *should* adhere to these ultimate standards is his personal affair; it involves will and conscience, not empirical knowledge.

Max Weber

Quoted in Edward Shils and Henry Finch, eds. *Max Weber on the Methodology of the Social Sciences.* New York: The Free Press. 1949.

Amid all crouched the freed slave, bewildered between friend and foe. He had emerged from slavery,—not the worst slavery in the world, not a slavery that made all life unbearable, rather a slavery that had here and there something of kindliness, fidelity, and happiness,—but withal slavery, which, so far as human aspiration and desert were concerned, classed the black man and the ox together. And the Negro knew full well that, whatever their deeper convictions may have been, Southern men had fought with desperate energy to perpetuate this slavery under which the black masses, with half-articulate thought, had writhed and shivered.

W.E.B. Du Bois

The Souls of Black Folk. New York: Dover Books. 1994.

The individual has become a mere cog in an enormous organization of things and powers which tear from his hands all progress, spirituality, and value in order to transform them from their subjective form into the form of a purely objective life. It needs merely to be pointed out that the metropolis is the genuine arena of this culture which outgrows all personal life. Here in buildings and educational institutions, in the wonders and comforts of space-conquering technology, in the formations of community life, and in the visible institutions of the state, is offered such an overwhelming fullness of crystallized and impersonalized spirit that the personality, so to speak, cannot maintain itself under its impact.

Georg Simmel

The Metropolis and Mental Life. Quoted in David Frisby and Mike Featherstone, eds. *Simmel on Culture.* Taken from Hans Gerth trans. and Kurt H. Wolff ed. *The Sociology of Georg Simmel.* Glencoe: Free Press. 1950.

On the one hand, life is made infinitely easy for the personality in that stimulations, interests, uses of time and consciousness are offered to it from all sides. They carry the person as if in a stream, and one needs hardly to swim for oneself. On the other hand, however, life is composed more and more of these impersonal contents and offerings which tend to displace the genuine personal colorations and incomparabilities. This results in the individual's summoning the utmost in uniqueness and particularization, in order to preserve his most personal core. He has to exaggerate this personal element in or to remain audible even to himself.

Georg Simmel

The Metropolis and Mental Life. Quoted in David Frisby and Mike Featherstone, eds. *Simmel on Culture.* In Hans Gerth trans. and Kurt H. Wolff ed. *The Sociology of Georg Simmel.* Glencoe: Free Press. 1950.

If we compare the relative progress African Americans have made in education and employment to the struggle to gain control over how we are represented, particularly in the mass media, we see that there has been little change in the area of representation. Opening a magazine or book, turning on the television set, watching a film, or looking at photographs in public spaces, we are most likely to see the images of black people that reinforce and reinscribe white supremacy. Those images may be constructed by white people who have not divested of racism or by people of color/black people who may see the world through the lens of white supremacy —internalized racism.

bell hooks
Black Looks: Race and Representation. Boston: South End Press. 1992.

In *Black Looks,* I critically interrogate old narratives, suggesting alternative ways to look at blackness, black subjectivity, and, of necessity, whiteness. While also exploring literature, music, and television, many of these essays focus on film. The emphasis on film is so central because it, more than any other media experience, determines how blackness and black people are seen and how other groups will respond to us based on their relation to these constructed and consumed images.

bell hooks
Black Looks: Race and Representation. Boston: South End Press. 1992.

We now live in a "recited" society that constantly circulates narratives and stories through the medium of mass communication. In the post-truth world, the consent of the audience, the difference between that explosion of messages that characterizes modernity is no longer stamped with the "authority" of their authors. De Certeau aptly describes the way in which old religious forms of authority have been supplanted by the plurality of narratives that empower the reader, rather than the writer…. The central paradox of modernity identified by…de Certeau is that the more information that is produced by the power bloc, the less it is able to govern the various interpretations made of it by socially situated subjects.

Nick Stevenson
Understanding Media Cultures: Social Theory and Mass Communication. London: Sage. 1985.

Many, often remarkable, works have sought to study the representations of a society, on the one hand, and its modes of behavior, on the other. Building on our knowledge of these social phenomena, it seems both possible and necessary to determine the *use* to which they are put by groups or individuals. For example, the analysis of the images broadcast by television (representation) and of the time spent watching television (behavior) should be complemented by a study of what the cultural consumer "makes" or "does" during this time with these images. The same goes for the use of urban space, the products purchased in the supermarket, the stories and legends distributed by the newspapers, and so on.

Michel de Certeau

The Practice of Everyday Lie. Trans. Seven Rendall. Berkeley, CA: University of California Press. 1984.

Recent analyses show that "every reading modifies its object," that (as Borges already pointed out) "one literature differs from another less by its text than by the way it is read," and that a system of verbal or iconic signs is a reservoir of forms to which the reader must give a meaning…. The reader takes neither the position of the author nor an author's position. He invents in texts something different from what they "intended." He detaches them from their (lost or accessory) origin. He combines their fragments and creates something un-known in the space organized by their capacity for allowing an indefinite plurality of meanings.

Michel de Certeau

The Practice of Everyday Lie. Trans. Seven Rendall. Berkeley, CA: University of California Press. 1984.

To understand individual experience one must study the social norms which make it possible…. Saussure, Freud, and Durkheim thus reverse the perspective which makes society the result of individual behavior and insist that behavior is made possible by collective social systems individuals have assimilated, consciously or unconsciously.

Jonathan Culler
Ferdinand de Saussure. Revised Edition. Ithaca, NY: Cornell University Press. 1986.

More than any other time in history, mankind faces a crossroads. One path leads to despair and utter hopelessness. The other, to total extinction. Let us pray we have the wisdom to choose correctly. I speak, by the way, now with any sense of futility, but with a panicky conviction of the absolute meaninglessness of existence, which could easily be interpreted as pessimism. It is not. It is merely a healthy concern for the predicament of modern man.

Woody Allen
Side Effects. New York: Ballantyne. 1981.

The word "myth" derives from the Greek mythos: "word," "speech," "tale of the gods." It can be defined as a narrative in which the characters are gods, heroes, and mystical beings, in which the plot is about the origin of things or about metaphysical events in human life, and in which the setting is a metaphysical world juxtaposed against the real world. In the beginning stages of human cultures, myths functioned as genuine "narrative theories" of the world. That is why all cultures have created them to explain their origins.

Marcel Danesi
Understanding Media Semiotics. London: Arnold. 2002.

The essence of fashion consists in the fact that it should always be exercised by only a part of a given group, the great majority of whom are merely on the road to adopting it. As soon as a fashion has been universally adopted, that is, as soon as anything that was originally done only by a few has really come to be practiced by all—as is the case in certain elements of clothing and in various forms of social conduct—we no longer characterize it as fashion. Every growth of a fashion drives it to its doom, because it thereby cancels out its distinctiveness.

Georg Simmel.
"The Philosophy of Fashion." In David Frisby and Mike Featherstone, eds. *Simmel on Culture*. London: Sage. 1997.

Fashion is indeed an unacknowledged world power. Even in the great clamor of world history, it guides man with a soft yet insistent voice. But again and again we feel its all-pervading presence and stare transfixed at the great public figures of the day who sometimes have themselves been carried to the top by the currents of fashion. Fashion is thus perhaps more powerful than all the other powers of the earth.

Rene Koenig
The Restless Image: A Sociology of Fashion. London: George Allen & Unwin. 1973.

Fashion has always advertised the person and "costumed the ego," as Edward Sapir said; but the tendency to extremes (ego screaming) and garishness and bad taste today suggest that it is doing more along these lines and less for its traditional function of class maintenance. Fashion is ceasing to be a hallmark by which classes can distinguish themselves and more a highly theatrical venture in identity.

Orrin E. Klapp
The Collective Search for Identity. New York: Holt, Rinehart and Winston. 1969.

The bread of full mechanization has the resiliency of a rubber sponge. When squeezed it returns to its former shape. The loaf becomes constantly whiter, more elastic, and frothier.... Since mechanization, it has often been pointed out, white bread has become much richer in fats, milk, and sugar. But these are added largely to stimulate sales by heightening the loaf's eye-appeal. The shortenings used in bread, a leading authority states, are "primarily for the purpose of imparting desirable tender eating or chewing qualities to the finished product." They produce the "soft velvet crumb," a cake-like structure, so that the bread is half-masticated, as it were, before reaching the mouth.

Sigfried Giedion
Mechanization Takes Command. New York: W.W. Norton. 1969.

McDonald's offers the hamburger without qualities for the man without qualities. It must be seen as more than a gaudy, vulgar oasis of tasteless ground meat, a fountain of sweet, syrupy malted milks in a big parking lot that caters to insolvent students, snack seekers, and hard-up hungers who grind its bloody gristle through their choppers at fifteen cents a shot. No! McDonalds is not just a hamburger joint...it is America, or, rather, it is the supreme triumph of all that is insane in American life.

Arthur Asa Berger
"McDonald's 'Evangelical' Hamburgers." *The Minnesota Daily.* 1964.

Like corruption, vodka is one of the indispensable lubricants of Russian life. The mere mention of vodka starts Russians salivating and puts them in a mellow mood. It would take an encyclopedia to explain all the vodka lore from the gentle tap under the throat which signifies drinking to the scores of ditties Russians have invented to convey the message, "let's go drink." Vodka eases the tension of life. It helps people to get to know each other, for many a Russian will say that he cannot trust another man until they have drunk seriously together. Vodka-drinking is invested with the symbolism of machismo.... Among working men and peasants, vodka is so popular that the $4.80 half-liter bottle is better than cash for odd jobs.

Hedrick Smith
The Russians. New York: Quadrangle/The New York Times Book Co. 1976.

Where does it come from, this vast blanket of things—coffee-pots and laptops, window fittings, lamps and fence finials, cars, hat pins, and hand trucks—that make up economies, mobilize desire, and so stir up controversy? The question leads to others because nothing stands alone—to understand any one thing you have to learn how it fits into larger arrays of physical objects, social sentiments, and ways of being. In the world of goods, as in worlds of any other sort, each element is just one interdependent fragment of a larger whole.

Harvey Moloch

Where Stuff Comes From: How Toasters, Toilets, Cars, Computers, and Many Other Things Come to Be As They Are. New York: Routledge. 2003.

The upshot is that status symbols are less often reminding people who they are and where they belong, and more often expressing a claim or wish to be somebody else. The range of material subject to fashion—that can be used as dramatic props, so to speak, for a new life—seems to be widening too: automobiles, gadgets, hobbies, foods, beverages, art, music, books, topics of conversation, slang, points of view, types of medical treatments—anything that can figure in one's life style as a status symbol.

Charles Winick

Desexualization in American Life. New Brunswick, NJ: Transaction Publications. 1995.

For a substantial number of women, the attractiveness of blondeness is less an opportunity to have more fun that the communication of a withdrawal of emotion, a lack of passion. One reason for Marilyn Monroe's enormous popularity was that she was less a tempestuous temptress than a nonthreatening child.... D.H. Lawrence pointed out that blonde women in American novels are often cool and unobtainable, while the dark women represent passion. Fictional blondes also tend to be vindictive and frigid.

Charles Winick

Desexualization in American Life. New Brunswick, NJ: Transaction Publications. 1995.

For Baudrillard, contemporary society is a postmodern society which is no longer structured by production in which the individual conforms to its needs but by symbolic exchange. It is a heterogeneous society of different groups with their own codes and practices of everyday life at the level of discourse, lifestyles, bodies, sexuality, communication, etc. and it involves the rejection of the logic of production and its instrumental rationality that dominated the modernist society of capitalism. Capitalism now has been replaced by a consumer society which is characterized by a proliferation of signs, the media and messages, environmental design, cybernetic steering systems, contemporary art and a sign culture. It is a society of simulations based on the new forms of technology and culture…. A world of hyper-reality is created in which everything in the world is simulated in the sense that models created by images replace the real.

David F. Walsh

"Subject/Object." In Chris Jenks, ed. *Core Sociological Dichotomies*. London: Sage. 1998.

The power of religious asceticism provided him [the bourgeois businessman]…with sober, conscientious, and unusually diligent workmen, who clung to their work as to a life purpose willed by God. Finally, it gave him the comforting assurance that the unequal distribution of the goods of this world was a special dispensation of Divine Providence, which in these differences, as in particular grace, pursued secret ends unknown to men.

Max Weber

The Protestant Ethic and the Spirit of Capitalism. New York: Scribners. 1958.

All known religious beliefs, whether simple or complex, present one common characteristic: they presuppose a classification of things, real and ideal, of which men think, into two classes or opposed groups, generally designated by two distinct terms which are translated well enough by the words *profane* and *sacred* (profane, sacré). This division of the world into two domains, the one containing all that is sacred, the other all that is profane, is the distinctive trait of religious thought.

Emile Durkheim

The Elementary Forms of Religious Life. New York: The Free Press. 1965.

Jean Baudrillard

Modern man spends less and less of his life in production within work and more and more of it in the production and continual innovation of his own needs and well being. He must constantly see to it that all his potentialities, all his consumer capacities are mobilized. If he forgets to do so, he will be gently and insistently reminded that he has no right not to be happy. It is not, then, true that he is passive. He is engaged in—has to engage in—continual activity. If not, he would run the risk of being content with what he has and become asocial. Hence the revival of a *universal curiosity*…in respect of cookery, culture, science, religion, sexuality, etc. "Try Jesus!" runs an American slogan. You have to try *everything* for consumerist man is haunted by the fear of "missing" something, some form of enjoyment or other.

Jean Baudrillard

The Consumer Society: Myths and Structures. London: Sage Publications. 1998.

Strong groups with numerous prescriptions that vary with social roles combine to form hierarchical collectivism. Strong groups whose members follow few prescriptions form an egalitarian culture, a shared life of voluntary consent, without coercion or inequality. Competitive individualism joins few prescriptions with weak group boundaries, thereby encouraging ever new combinations. When groups are weak and prescriptions strong, so that decisions are made for them by people on the outside, the controlled culture is fatalistic. The social idea of individualistic cultures is self-regulation.... Hierarchy is institutionalized authority.... Committed to a life of purely voluntary association, egalitarian cultures reject authority. An apathetic culture arises when people cannot control what happens to them. Since their boundaries are porous but the prescriptions imposed on them are severe, they develop fatalistic feelings.

Aaron Wildavsky

"Choosing preferences by constructing institutions: A cultural theory of preference formation." In A.A. Berger, ed. *Political Culture and Public Opinion.* New Brunswick, NJ: Transaction. 1989.

There is a universe of events that we smell and a universe that we hear; there is also a universe of events whose existence is embodied in photographs. Thus each year we eagerly await the official Chinese Communist May Day photograph to see who is photographed alongside the chairman and who has been displaced. The official photograph is not only a reflection of the political reality, but itself solidifies that reality and becomes an element in it. The question, therefore, is to what degree events that exist in photographs exert an effect outside the photographs. Does a photograph act back on and shape the real world?

Stanley Milgram

"The Image Freezing Machine." *Society.* November/December 1976.

It is some comfort for the little man who has become expelled from the Horatio Alger dream, who despairs of penetrating the thicket of grand strategy in politics and business, to see his heroes as a lot of guys who like or dislike highballs, cigarettes, tomato juice, golf and social gatherings—just like himself. He knows how to converse in the sphere of consumption and here he can make no mistakes. By narrowing his focus of attention, he can experience the gratification of being confirmed in his own pleasures and discomforts by participating in the pleasures and discomforts of the great.

Leo Lowenthal

"Biographies in Popular Magazines." In P.F. Lazarsfeld and F. Stanton, eds. *Radio Research 1942-43*. New York: Duell, Sloan & Pearce. 1944.

We have to make a radical shift away from thinking about consumption as a manifestation of individual choices.... Culture itself is the result of myriads of individual choices, not primarily between commodities but between kinds of relationships. The basic choice a rational individual has to make is the choice about what kind of society to live in. According to that choice, the rest follows. Artefacts are selected to demonstrate that choice. Food is eaten, clothes are worn, cinema, books, music, holidays, all the rest are choices that conform with the initial choice of for a form of society.

Mary Douglas

"In Defence of Shopping." In Pasi Falk and Colin Campbell, eds. *The Shopping Experience*. London: Sage Publications. 1997.

In Baxter's view the care for external goods should only lie on the shoulders of the "saint like a light cloak, which can be thrown aside at any moment." But fate decreed that the cloak should become an iron cage. Since asceticism undertook to remodel the world and to work out its ideals in the world, material goods have gained an increasing and finally an inexorable power over the lives of men as at no previous period in history.

Max Weber

The Protestant Ethic and the Spirit of Capitalism. Trans. Talcott Parsons. New York: Charles Scribner's Sons. 1958.

The research of sociologists and anthropologists...has shown that girls and boys learn to use language differently in the sex-separate peer groups. Typically, a girl has a best friend with whom she sits and talks, frequently telling secrets. It's the telling of secrets, the fact and the way that they talk to each other, that makes them best friends. For boys, activities are central: their best friends are the ones they do things with. Boys also tend to play in larger groups that are hierarchical. High-status boys give orders and push low-status boys around. So boys are expected to seize center stage: by exhibiting their skill, displaying their knowledge, and challenging and resisting challenges.

Deborah Tannen

"Teacher's Classroom Strategies Should Recognize that Men and Women Use Language Differently." *The Chronicle of Higher Education.* June 19, 1991.

Branded lifestyles are not merely superficial veneers on deeper identities but have to some degree become substitute identities— forms of acquired character that have the potential to go all the way down to the core. They displace traditional ethnic and cultural traits and overwhelm the voluntary aspects of identity we choose for ourselves.

Benjamin Barber

Consumed: How Markets Corrupt Children, Infantalize Adults, and Swallow Citizens Whole. New York: W.W. Norton, 2007.

Rather than unreflexively adopting a lifestyle, through tradition or habit, the new heroes of consumer culture make lifestyle a life project and display their individuality and sense of style in the particularity of the assemblage of goods, clothes, practices, experiences, appearance and bodily dispositions they design together into a lifestyle. The modern individual within consumer culture is made conscious that he speaks not only with his clothes, but with his home, furnishings, decoration, car and other activities which are to be read and classified in terms of the presence and absence of taste. This preoccupation with customizing a lifestyle and a stylistic self-consciousness are not just to be found among the young and the affluent.

Mike Featherstone

Consumer Culture & Postmodernism. London: Sage Publications. 1991.

Any analysis of the system of objects must ultimately imply an analysis of discourse about objects—that is to say, an analysis of promotional "messages" (comprising image and discourse). For advertising is not simply an adjunct to the system of objects; it cannot be detached there from, nor can it be restricted to its "proper" function (there is no such thing as advertising strictly confined to the supplying of information). This lack of proportion is the "functional" apotheosis of the system. Advertising in its entirety contributes a useless and unnecessary universe. It is pure connotation. It contributes nothing to production or to the direct practical application of things, yet it plays an integral part in the system of objects not merely because it relates to consumption but also because it itself becomes an object to be consumed.

Jean Baudrillard

The System of Objects. London: Verso. 1996.

Here at last is the expert analysis that will help you capture your share of the nearly $100 billion that teenagers spend. This book explains where teenagers get their money, how and why they spend it, and what they think about themselves and the world around them. It presents five rules that will make your advertising more appealing to teens. Learn about brands teens think are cool, words to use in advertising to teens, which media and promotions teens prefer, and how much influence teens have over what their parents buy. This is a fascinating look into the world of teens—a market whose income is almost all discretionary.

Peter Zollo

Wise Up to Teens: Insights into Marketing and Advertising to Teenagers. Ithaca, NY: New Strategist Publications. 1999.

PRIZM operates on the principle that "birds of a feather flock together." It's a worldwide phenomenon that people with similar cultural backgrounds, needs, and perspectives naturally gravitate toward one another, choose to live in neighborhoods offering affordable advantages and compatible lifestyles. That's why, for instance, many young career singles and couples choose dynamic urban neighborhoods like Chicago's Gold Coast, while families with children prefer the suburbs which offer more affordable housing, convenient shopping, and strong local schools.

Claritas

website: www.claritas.com

It's important for brands to be aware of the complexities and contradictions around the Consumer Narcissus. Consumer culture encourages consumers to think of themselves as special, unique and wonderful people. But this process, sometimes fuelled by forms of over literal market research, can lead to a consumer tyranny wherein the hapless brand abandons core equities in knee-jerk responses to the whims of their consumer masters. We can never fully please the consumer. And this, ironically, is the key to the survival of the consumer economy. Consumer culture has constructed people that can never be fully satisfied by anything. But this infinite extension of desire is one of the pre-conditions for consumer culture to work effectively. We need for people to be relatively

Greg Rowland

happy with their purchases, but not so happy that they don't continually explore new avenues of self-fulfilment through consumption.

Greg Rowland
"Brand Narcissism." www.Semiotics.co.UK/index.html

It has been observed by critics of the American mass media that the method used in television commercials is never [to] present an ordered, sequential, rational argument but simply [to] present the product associated with desirable things, or attitudes. Thus Coca-Cola is shown held by a beautiful blonde, who sits in a Cadillac, surrounded by bronze, muscular admirers, with the sun shining overhead. By repetition, these elements become associated in our minds, into a pattern of sufficient cohesion, so that one element can magically evoke the others.

Raphael Patai
Myth and Modern Man. Englewood Cliffs, NJ: Prentice-Hall. 1972.

Marxist Theory

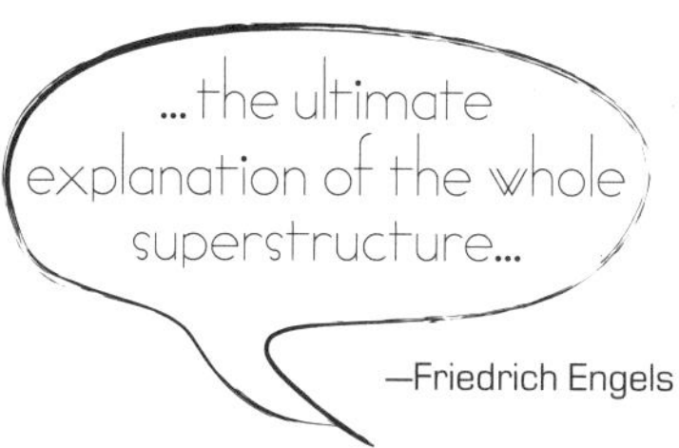

Marxist theories, along with semiotic theory, psychoanalytic theory, and sociological theory, are the basic theories which inform the field of cultural studies. Consider the French culture critic Jean Baudrillard, who figured prominently in the last chapter. He combines semiotics, psychoanalytic theory and Marxism in his writings, using concepts from each field when they are most relevant. Many prominent Marxists are also semioticians, such as Roland Barthes. So we must expect to find all kinds of different combinations of theories in the work of cultural studies scholars and writers.

Marxist theories offer a powerful tool for analyzing the way the "ruling classes," those who control the economic institutions of society, shape the consciousness of the masses, what Marx called "the proletariat." He focused upon the class makeup of societies and of the way those at the top of the socio-economic pyramid maintained their position of dominance. We find Marxist theories informing the work of the French critic Henri Lefebvre, the English critic John Berger, the German critic Walter Benjamin, and numerous other culture analysts. Although modern-day Marxists may not believe in violent revolution and other ideas of Marx, they still use his concepts to offer their critiques of the deficiencies of contemporary bourgeois capitalist societies.

The ideas of the ruling class are, in every age, the ruling ideas: i.e. the class which is the dominant material force in society is at the same time the dominant intellectual force. The class which has the means of material production at its disposal, has control at the same time over the means of mental production.

Karl Marx

Selected Writings in Sociology and Social Philosophy. Trans. T.B. Bottomore. New York: McGraw-Hill. 1964.

The history of all hitherto existing societies is the history of class struggles. Freeman and slave, patrician and plebeian, lord and serf, guild-master and journeyman, in a word oppressor and oppressed, stood in constant opposition to one another, carried on an uninterrupted, now hidden, now open, fight, a fight that each time ended either in a revolutionary reconstitution of society at large, or in the common ruin of the contending classes.

Karl Marx

Selected Writings in Sociology and Social Philosophy. Trans. T.B. Bottomore. New York: McGraw-Hill. 1964.

The economic structure of society always furnishes the real basis, starting from which we can alone work out the ultimate explanation of the whole superstructure of juridical and political institutions as well as of the religious, philosophical, and other ideas of a given historical period.

Friedrich Engels

Socialism: Utopian and Scientific. In R. Tucker, ed. *The Marx-Engels Reader.* New York: W.W. Norton. 1972.

Rigid institutionalism transforms modern mass culture into a medium of undreamed psychological control. The repetitiveness, the selfsameness, and the ubiquity of modern mass culture tend to make for automatized reactions and to weaken the forces of individual resistance.

Theodor W. Adorno
Philosophy of Modern Music. New York: Seabury. 1948.

The overthrow of bourgeois rule can be accomplished only by the proletariat, as the particular class, which, by the economic conditions of its existence, is being prepared for this work and is provided with the opportunity and the power to perform it.... The doctrine of the class struggle, as applied by Marx to the question of the state and of the Socialist revolution, leads inevitably to the recognition of the *political rule* of the proletariat, of its dictatorship, *i.e.,* of a power shared with none and relying directly upon the armed force of the masses. The overthrow of the bourgeoisie is realisable only by the transformation of the proletariat into the *ruling class,* able to crush the inevitable and desperate resistance of the bourgeoisie, and to organise, for the new economic order, *all* the toiling and exploited masses.

Vladimir Lenin
State and Revolution. New York: International Publishers. 1932.

The alienation of the worker from his product means not only that his labour becomes an object, takes on its own existence, but that it exists outside him, independently, and alien to him, and that it stands opposed to him as an autonomous power. The life which he has given to the object sets itself against him as an alien and hostile force.

Karl Marx
Selected Writings in Sociology and Social Philosophy. Trans. T.B. Bottomore. New York: McGraw-Hill. 1964.

Every man speculates upon creating a new need in another in order to force him to a new sacrifice, to place him in a new dependence, and to entice him into a new kind of pleasure and thereby into economic ruin. Everyone tries to establish over others an alien power in order to find there the satisfaction of his own egoistic need.

Karl Marx

Karl Marx: Early Writings. T.B. Bottomore, ed. and trans. New York: McGraw-Hill. 1963.

The Marxist method, recently in varying degrees of combination with structuralism and semiology, has provided an incisive analytic tool for studying the political signification in every facet of contemporary culture, including popular entertainment in TV and films, music, mass circulation books, newspaper and magazine features, comics, fashion, tourism, sports and games, as well as such acculturating institutions as education, religion, the family and child-rearing...all the patterns of work, play, and other customs of everyday life.

Donald Lazere

"Mass culture, political consciousness and English studies." *College English.*, 1977.

Walter Benjamin

The authenticity of a thing is the essence of all that is transmissible from its beginning, ranging from its substantive duration to its testimony to the history which it has experienced. Since the historical testimony rests on the authenticity, the former, too, is jeopardized by reproduction when substantive duration ceases to matter. And what is really jeopardized when the historical testimony is affected is the authority of the object. One might subsume the eliminated element in the term "aura" and go on to say: that which withers in the age of mechanical reproduction is the aura of the work of art. This is a symptomatic process whose significance points beyond the realm of art. One might generalize by saying: the technique of reproduction detaches the reproduced object from the domain of tradition.

Walter Benjamin

"The Work of Art in the Age of Mechanical Reproduction." In G. Mast and M. Cohen, eds. *Film Theory and criticism: Introductory readings.* Oxford: Oxford University Press. 1974.

It takes possession of art, literature, all available signifiers and vacant signifieds; it is art and literature, it gleans the leavings of the Festival to recondition them for its own ends.... Publicity [advertising] acquires the significance of an ideology, the ideology of trade and replaces what was once philosophy, ethics, religion and aesthetics.

Henri Lefebvre

Everyday Life in the Modern World. Trans. Sacha Rabinovich. New Brunswick, NJ: Transaction Publications. 1984.

The time is past when advertising tried to condition the consumer by the repetition of slogans; today the more subtle forms of publicity represent a whole attitude to life; if you know how to choose you will choose this brand and no other…you are being looked after, cared for, told how to live better, how to dress fashionably, how to decorate your house, in short, how to exist; you are totally and thoroughly programmed, except that you still have to choose between so many good things.

Henri Lefebvre

Everyday Life in the Modern World. Trans. Sacha Rabinovich. New Brunswick, NJ: Transaction Publications. 1984.

The way we see things is affected by what we know or what we believe…. We only see what we look at. To look is an act of choice. As a result of this act, what we see is brought within our reach—though not necessarily within arm's reach. To touch something is to situate oneself in relation to it…. We never look at just one thing; we are always looking at the relation between things and ourselves. Our vision is continually active, continually moving, constituting what is present to us as we are.

John Berger
Ways of Seeing. London: British Broadcasting System and Penguin. 1978.

Every image embodies a way of seeing. Even a photograph. For photographs are not, as is often assumed, a mechanical record. Every time we look at a photograph, we are aware, however slightly, of the photographer selecting that sight from an infinity of other possible sights. This is true even in the most casual family photograph…. Images were first made to conjure up the appearance of something that was absent. Gradually it became evident that an image could outlast what it represented; it then showed how something or somebody had once looked…. An image became a record of how X had seen Y…. No other kind or relic or text from the past can offer such a direct testimony about the world which surrounded other people at other times. In this respect, images are more precise and richer than literature.

John Berger
Ways of Seeing. London: British Broadcasting System and Penguin. 1978.

In contrast to liberal feminists, socialist feminists, as Marxists, assume that the class system under capitalism is fundamentally responsible for women's oppression. At the same time they agree with radical feminists that "patriarchy" (gender oppression) is fundamental in its own right and certainly existed long before capitalism. Thus, most socialist feminists argue that patriarchy and capitalism must be simultaneously addressed, largely via the eradication of divided labor by both gender and class....Also, in contrast to liberal feminists' focus on how media affects individual attitudes and behaviors, socialist feminists emphasize the centrality of media (and other communication processes, such as language, education and art) in actually constructing ideology, including the ideology of women's secondary status.

H. Leslie Steeves and Marilyn Crafton Smith

"Observations from a Socialist Feminist Perspective." *Journal of Communication Inquiry*. Vol. 11, Number 1,Winter 1987.

A terrorist society is the logical and structural outcome of an over-repressive society; compulsion and the illusion of freedom converge; unacknowledged compulsion besiege the lives of communities (and of their individual members).... In a terrorist society terror is diffuse, violence is always latent, pressure is exerted from all sides on its members who can only avoid it and shift its weight by a super-human effort; each member is a terrorist because he wants to be in power (if only briefly); thus there is no need for a dictator; each member betrays and chastises himself. Terror cannot be located, for it comes from everywhere and from every specific thing.

Henri Lefebvre

Everyday Life in the Modern World. Trans. Sacha Rabinovich. New Brunswick, NJ: Transaction Publications. 1984.

The work of Kafka...has been subjected to a mass ravishment by no less than three armies of interpreters. Those who read Kafka as a social allegory see case studies of the frustrations and insanity of modern bureaucracy and its ultimate issuance in the totalitarian state. Those who read Kafka as a psychoanalytic allegory see desperate revelations of Kafka's fear of his father, his castration anxieties, his sense of his own impotence, his thralldom to his dreams. Those who read Kafka as a religious allegory explain that K. in *The Castle* is trying to gain access to heaven, that Joseph

K. in *The Trial* is being judged by the inexorable and mysterious justice of God.... It should be noted that interpretation is not simply the compliment that mediocrity pays to genius. It is, indeed, *the* modern way of understanding something, and is applied to works of every quality.

Susan Sontag

Against Interpretation. New York: Laurel Books. 1969.

Does advertising create the need, does it, in the pay of capitalist producers, shape desire? Be this as it may, advertising is unquestionably a powerful instrument; is it not the first of consumer goods and does it not provide consumption with its paraphernalia of signs, images and pattern? Is it not the rhetoric of our society, permeating social languages, literature and imagination with its ceaseless intrusions upon our daily experience and our more intimate aspirations? Is it not on the way to becoming the main *ideology* of our time, and is not this fact confirmed by the importance of propaganda modelled on advertising methods?

Henri Lefebvre

Everyday Life in the Modern World. Trans. Sacha Rabinovich. New Brunswick, NJ: Transaction Publications. 1984.

1.

In societies where the modern conditions of production prevail, all of life presents itself as an immense accumulation of *spectacles.* Everything that was directly lived has moved away into a representation.

2.

The images detached from every aspect of life fuse into a common stream in which the unity of this life can no longer be reestablished. Reality considered *partially* unfolds, in its own general unity, as a pseudo-world *apart,* an object of mere contemplation. The specialization of images of the world is completed in the world of the autonomous image, where the liar has lied to himself. The spectacle in general, as the concrete inversion of life, is the autonomous movement of the non-living.

3.

The spectacle is not a collection of images, but a social relation among people, mediated by images.

Guy Debord

Society of the Spectacle. Michigan: Black and Red. 1967.

Our Latin American countries become trash cans being constantly repainted for the voyeuristic and orgiastic pleasures of the metropolitan nations. Every day, this very minute, television, radio, magazines, newspapers, cartoons, newscasts, films, clothing, and records, from the dignified gab of history textbooks to the trivia of daily conversation, all contribute to weakening the international solidarity of the oppressed. We Latin Americans are separated from each other by the vision we have acquired of each other via the comics and the other mass culture media. This vision is nothing less than our own reduced and distorted image.

Ariel Dorfman and A. Mattelart

How To Read Donald Duck: Imperialist Ideology in the Disney Comic.
Second Edition. New York: International General. 1984.

Williams is often interpreted as one of the precursors and key sources of British cultural studies that first emerged in the early 1960s and that has since become a global phenomenon. Developing an expanded conception of culture that went beyond the literary conceptions dominant in the British academy, Williams conceptualized culture as "a whole way of life," that encompasses cultural artifacts, modes of sensibility, values and practices.... Arguing for the need to think together "culture and society," seeing the importance of media culture, and overcoming the division between "high" and "low" culture, Williams produced an impressive series of publications that deeply influenced the trajectory of British cultural studies.

Meenakshi Gigi Durham and Douglas M. Kellner, eds.
Media and Cultural Studies: KeyWorks. Malden, MA: Blackwell. 2001.

The major modern communications systems are now so evidently key institutions in advanced capitalist societies that they require the same kind of attention...that is given to the institutions of industrial production and distribution.

Raymond Williams
Marxism and Literature. Oxford: Oxford University Press. 1977.

The complex sociology of actual audiences, highly variable systems (the cinema audience, the newspaper readership, and the television audience being highly distinct social structures), is overlaid by bourgeois norms of "cultural producers" and "the mass public," with the additional effect that the complex sociology of these producers as managers and agents within capitalist systems, is itself not developed.

Raymond Williams
Marxism and Literature. Oxford: Oxford University Press. 1977.

For if we have learned to see the relation of any cultural work to what we have learned to call a "sign-system" (and this has been the important contribution of cultural semiotics), we can also come to see that a sign-system is itself a specific structure of social relationships "internally," in that the signs depend on, were formed in, relationships "externally," in that the system depends on, is formed in, the institutions which activate it (and which are then at once cultural and social and economic institutions).

Raymond Williams
Marxism and Literature. Oxford: Oxford University Press. 1977.

For "hegemony" is a concept which at once includes and goes beyond two powerful earlier concepts, that of "culture" as a "whole social process," in which men define and shape their whole lives; and that of "ideology," in any of its Marxist senses, in which a system of meanings and values is the expression or projection of a particular class interest.

Raymond Williams

Marxism and Literature. Oxford: Oxford University Press. 1977.

It [hegemony] is a whole body of practices and expectations, over the whole of living: our senses and assignments of energy, our shaping perceptions of ourselves and our world. It is a lived system of meanings and values—constitutive and constituting—which as they are experienced as practices appear as reciprocally confirming. It thus

Raymond Williams

constitutes a sense of reality for most people in society, a sense of absolute because experienced reality beyond which it is very difficult for most members in the society to move, in most areas of their lives.

Raymond Williams

Marxism and Literature. Oxford: Oxford University Press. 1977.

"Everyday life" refers to dull routine, the ongoing go-to-work, pay-the-bills, homeward trudge of daily existence. It indicates a sense of being in the world beyond philosophy, virtually beyond the capacity of language to describe, that we simply know as the grey reality enveloping all we do.... The "modern world" refers to the products of industrialization and the controls necessary to socialize workers and regulate consumption. It is a society whose rational character is defined through and has its limits set by highly organized groups (bureaucracies) operating through the state and/or the corporate state; whose purpose lies less in production than in consumption; whose level of operation takes place on and is aimed at influencing everyday life. In this way Lefebvre joins together technological, consumer, affluent, and leisure activities emphasized by other social theorists, into what he calls a society of bureaucratically controlled consumption.

Phil Wander

"Introduction." In Henri Lefebvre. *Everyday Life in the Modern World.* Trans. Sacha Rabinovich. New Brunswick, NJ: Transaction Publications. 1984.

People's responses to their objective class situation gives rise to the secondary notion of class for itself. This is the (sometimes only potential) awareness among people of a common identity springing from their common experience.

John Fiske and John Hartley

Reading Television. London: Methuen. 1978.

The worker...feels himself at home only during his leisure, whereas at work he feels homeless. His work is not voluntary but imposed, forced labour. It is not the satisfaction of a need, but only a means for satisfying other needs. Its alien character is clearly shown by the fact that as soon as there is no physical or other compulsion it is avoided like the plague…. The alienation of the worker in his product means not only that his labour becomes an object, takes on its own existence, but that it exists outside him, independently, and alien to him, and that it stands opposed to him as an autonomous power. The life which he has given to the objects sets itself against him as an alien and hostile force.

Karl Marx

Selected Writings in Sociology and Social Philosophy. Trans. T. B. Bottomore. New York: McGraw-Hill. 1964.

Morality, religion, metaphysics and other ideologies, and their corresponding forms of consciousness, no longer retain therefore their appearance of an autonomous existence. They have no history, no development; it is men, who in developing their material production and their material intercourse, change, along with this their real existence, their thinking and the products of their thinking. Life is not determined by consciousness, but consciousness by life.

Karl Marx

Selected Writings in Sociology and Social Philosophy. Trans. T.B. Bottomore. New York: McGraw-Hill. 1964.

Things are never as they seem in class societies, Marx tells us, because exploitation must be disguised for the social order to be sustained. Since rulers do not like to think of themselves as exploiters, benefiting unjustly from the labor of others, and the exploited must be kept ignorant of their subjection lest they revolt, the truth must be kept from both rulers and ruled alike…. In Volume 3 of *Capital,* Marx voiced his belief that "all science would be superfluous if the manifest form and the essence of things directly coincided." Implicit in this statement, as G.A. Cohen has shown in a lovely appendix called "Karl Marx and the Withering Away of Social Science," is the belief that all social science would cease to be necessary in a socialist society, because socialism, unlike capitalism, would not be based on deception."

Michael Thompson, Richard Ellis and Aaron Wildavsky

Cultural Theory. Boulder, CO: Westview Press. 1990.

In the second half of the twentieth century in Europe, or at any rate in France, there is nothing—whether object, individual or social group—that is valued apart from its double, the image that advertises and sanctifies it. This image duplicates not only any object's material, perceptible existence but desire and pleasure that it makes into fictions situating them in the land of make-believe, promising "happiness"—the happiness of being a consumer.

Henri Lefebvre

Everyday Life in the Modern World. Trans. Sacha Rabinovich. New Brunswick, NJ: Transaction Publications. 1984.

The art of any period tends to serve the ideological interests of the ruling class. If we were simply saying that European art, between 1600 and 1900 served the interest of the successive ruling classes, all of whom depended in different ways on the new power of capital, we should not be saying anything very new. What is being proposed is a little more precise: that a way of seeing the world which was ultimately determined by new attitudes to property and exchange, found its visual expression in the oil painting and could not have found it in any other visual art form. Oil painting did to appearances what capital did to social relations. It reduced everything to the equality of objects.

John Berger

Ways of Seeing. New York: Penguin. 1972.

For masses of black women, the political reality that underlies Madonna's and our recognition that this is a society where "blondes" not only "have more fun" but where they are more likely to succeed in any endeavor is white supremacy and racism. We cannot see Madonna's change in hair color as being merely a question of aesthetic choice. I agree with Julie Burchell in her critical work *Girls on Film,* when she reminds us: "What does it say about racial purity when the best blondes have all been brunettes (Harlow, Monroe, Bardot)? I think it says that we are not as white as we think. I think it says that Pure is a Bore." I also know that it is the expressed desire of the non-blonde Other for those characteristics that are seen as the quintessential markers of racial aesthetic superiority that perpetuate and uphold white supremacy. In this sense Madonna has much in common with the masses of black women who suffer from internalized racism and are forever terrorized by a standard of beauty they feel they can never truly embody.

bell hooks

Black Looks: Race and Representation. Boston: South End Press. 1992

The ideological processes that determine political candidates as well as products are hidden, argue critical scholars. Media influence, for Hall and for neo-Marxist scholars in general, is not in overt "messages" but in the ideological structuring or values and beliefs that shape or constrain the message. Ideology is evidenced in the taken for granted, the assumed, the "common sense" of a situation; it is what is not said, because it "goes without saying." It works by excluding what cannot be imagined or thought because it seems too bizarre or absurd or beyond the pale.

Joli Jensen

Redeeming Modernity: Contradictions in Media Criticism. London: Sage. 1990.

Postmodernist Theory

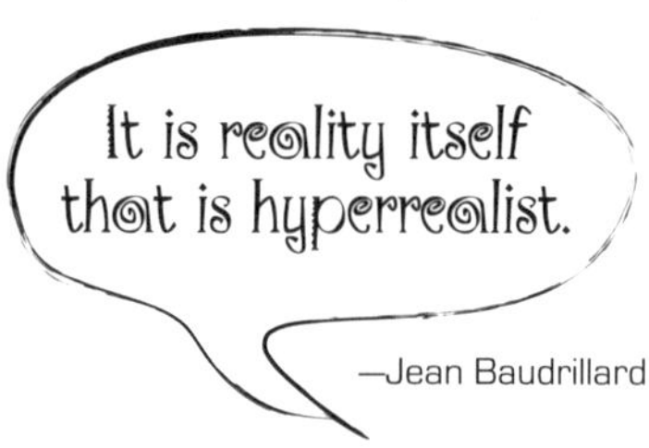

The term "postmodernism" suggests something coming after modernism, which was the philosophical and aesthetic cultural dominant until approximately 1960, some postmodern theorists argue. Around 1960 there was a huge cultural shift, and the philosophical system we call postmodernism took control of life. The term has been described by a postmodern theorist, Jean-François Lyotard, as "incredulity toward metanarratives," which means that the old overarching philosophical systems that shaped our beliefs, such as liberalism and a belief in progress, were jettisoned, and people created their own micro-narratives, which shaped their lives. The problem was that without anything to guide people, they became erratic, and there was a crisis of legitimation. What is the right thing to do if you have no philosophical or religious belief to guide you?

The impact of postmodernism was reflected in architecture, the arts, philosophy and other aspects of everyday life. Postmodern societies have been characterized as more focused on simulacra than "the real thing," and as being dominated by consumer cultures. One prominent postmodern critic argues that postmodernism is just another name for an evolved form of capitalism. I have written a mystery novel, *Postmortem for a Postmodernist*, which explores different approaches to postmodernism and written another book, *The Portable Postmodernist,* which deals with the theories of a number of postmodernist theorists and cultural critics.

Simplifying to the extreme, I define postmodern as incredulity toward metanarratives. This incredulity is undoubtedly a product of progress in the sciences: but that progress in turn presupposes it. To the obsolescence of the metanarrative apparatus of legitimation corresponds, most notably, the crisis of metaphysical philosophy and of the university institution which in the past relied on it. The narrative function is losing its functors, its great hero, its great dangers, its great voyages, its great goal.

Jean-François Lyotard

The Postmodern Condition: A Report on Knowledge. Minneapolis: University of Minnesota Press. 1984.

America is neither dream nor reality. It is a hyperreality.... Everything here is real and pragmatic, and yet is the stuff of dreams too. It may be that the truth of America can only be seen by a European, since he alone will discover here the perfect simulacrum—that of the immanence and material transcription of all values. The Americans, for their part, have no sense of simulation. They are themselves simulation in its most developed state, but they have no language in which to describe it, since they themselves are the model.

Jean Baudrillard

America. London: Verso. 1988.

One of the concerns frequently aroused by periodizing hypotheses is that these tend to obliterate difference and to project the idea of the historical period as massive homogeneity (bounded on either side by inexplicable chronological metamorphoses and punctuation marks). This is, however, why it seems to me essential to grasp postmodernism not as a style but rather as a cultural dominant.

Fredric Jameson

Postmodernism or, The Cultural Logic of Late Capitalism. Durham, NC: Duke University Press. 1991.

In the most restricted sense, modernism points to the styles we associate with the artistic movements which originated around the turn of the century and which have dominated the various arts until recently. Figures frequently cited are: Joyce, Yeats, Gide, Proust, Rilke, Kafka, Mann, Musil, Lawrence and Faulkner in literature; Rilke, Pound, Eliot, Lorca, Valery in poetry; Strindberg and Pirandello in drama; Matisse, Picasso, Braque, Cézanne and the Futurist, Expressionist, Dada and Surrealist movements in painting; Stravinsky, Schoenberg and Berg in music.

Mike Featherstone

Consumer Culture & Postmodernism. London: Sage Publications. 1991.

Utopia…poses its own specific problem of any theory of the postmodern and any periodization of it. For according to one conventional view, postmodernism is also at one with the definitive "end of ideologies," a development announced (along with "postindustrial society") by the conservative ideologues of the fifties (Daniel Bell, Lipset, etc.) "disproven" dramatically by the sixties, only to "come true" in the seventies and eighties. "Ideology" in this sense meant Marxism, and its "end" went hand in hand with the end of Utopia, already secured by the great postwar anti-Stalinist dystopias, such as *1984*. But "Utopia" in that period was also a code word that simply meant "socialism" or any

Fredric Jameson

revolutionary attempt to create a radically different society.

Fredric Jameson

Postmodernism or, The Cultural Logic of Late Capitalism. Durham, NC: Duke University Press. 1991.

Jameson claims that each stage of capitalism has a corresponding cultural style. Hence, realism, modernism, and postmodernism are the cultural levels of market capitalism, monopoly capitalism, and multinational capitalism. In characterizing postmodernism as the cultural dominant of late capitalism, Jameson also employs Raymond Williams'…distinction between emergent and dominant cultural forms and provides a more radical account of postmodernism as a historical rupture than do radical postmodernists…. In his essay "Postmodernism and Consumer Society," (1983), Jameson states "Radical breaks between periods do not generally involve complete changes of content, but rather the restructuration of a certain number of elements already given; features that were subordinate now become dominant, and features that had been dominant again become secondary."

Steven Best and Douglas Kellner

Postmodern Theory: Critical Interrogations. New York: Guilford Press. 1991.

There is a good deal of debate about how far back into the nineteenth century modernism should be taken (some would want to go back to the bohemian avant-garde of the 1830s). The basic features of modernism can be summarized as: an aesthetic self-consciousness and reflexiveness; a rejection of narrative structure in favour of simultaneity and montage; an exploration of the paradoxical, ambiguous and uncertain open-ended nature of reality; and a rejection of the notion of an integrated personality in favour of an emphasis upon the de-structured, de-humanized subject.

Mike Featherstone
Consumer Culture & Postmodernism. London: Sage Publications. 1991.

As opposed to the seriousness of "high modernism," postmodernism exhibited a new insouciance, a new playfulness, and a new eclecticism embodied above all in Andy Warhol's "pop art" but also manifested in celebrations of Las Vegas architecture, found objects, happenings, Nam June Paik's video-installations, underground film, and the novels of Thomas Pynchon. In opposition to the well-wrought, formally sophisticated, and aesthetically demanding modernist art, postmodernist art was fragmentary and eclectic, mixing forms from "high culture" and "popular culture," subverting aesthetic boundaries and expanding the domain of art to encompass the images of advertising, the kaleidoscopic mosaics of television, the experiences of the post holocaust nuclear age, and an always proliferating consumer capitalism.

Douglas Kellner
"Postmodernism as Social Theory: some Challenges and Problems."
Theory, Culture & Society . Vol. 5, Nos. 2-3, June 1988.

A postmodern artist or writer is in the position of a philosopher: the text he writes, the work he produces are not in principle governed by preestablished rules and they cannot be judged according to a determining judgment, by applying familiar categories to the text or to the work. Those rules and categories are what the work of art itself is looking for. The artist and the writer, then, are working without rules in order to formulate the rules of what *will have been done.* Hence the fact that work and text have the character of an *event*; hence also, they always come too late for their author, or, what amounts to the same thing, their being put into work, their realization (*mise en oeuvre*) always begins too soon. *Post modern* would have to be understood according to the paradox of the future: (*post*) anterior (*modo*).

Jean-François Lyotard

The Postmodern Condition: A Report on Knowledge. Minneapolis: University of Minnesota Press. 1984.

"America is the most well-developed postmodern society," Fess went on, gazing into the middle distance, "and all of us who are interested in what the future holds are drawn irresistibly, as a moth is to a flame, to America. And what's most interesting is that Americans don't know what they've done, don't realize that in their invincible ignorance, they have created the quintessential postmodern society. That is why French sociologists and philosophers are so important. We have a history of explaining America to Americans. I and my colleagues, in a sense, are descendents of de Tocqueville. For the twentieth century, though."

Arthur Asa Berger

Postmortem for a Postmodernist. Walnut Creek, CA: AltaMira Press. 1997.

It is reality itself that is hyperrealist. Surrealism's secret already was that the most banal reality could become surreal, but only in certain privileged moments that are still nevertheless connected with art and the imaginary. Today it is quotidian reality in its entirety—political, social, historical and economic—that from now on incorporates the simulating dimension of hyperrealism. We live everywhere already in a "aesthetic hallucination of reality."

Jean Baudrillard

Simulations. New York: Semiotext(e). 1983.

A postmodern artist or writer is in the position of a philosopher: the text he writes, the work he produces are not in principle governed by preestablished rules and they cannot be judged according to a determining judgment, by applying familiar categories to the text or to the work. Those rules and categories are what the work of art itself is looking for. The artist and the writer, then, are working without rules in order to formulate the rules of what *will have been done*. Hence the fact that work and text have the character of an *event*; hence also, they always come too late for their author, or, what amounts to the same thing, their being put into work, their realization (*mise en oeuvre*) always begin too soon. *Post modern* would have to be understood according to the paradox of the future: (*post*) anterior (*modo*).

Jean-François Lyotard
The Postmodern Condition: A Report on Knowledge. Minneapolis: University of Minnesota Press. 1984.

In contradistinction to the teleological, absolute, and single-minded Romantic narrative of "grand amour," the affair is a cultural form that attempts to immobilize and repeat, compulsively, the primordial experience of "novelty." During the Victorian era, people chose from a very narrow pool of available partners and often felt compelled to marry their first suitor. The contemporary affair, by contrast, presupposes variety and freedom to choose. This "shop-and-choose" outlook is due to a much wider pool of available partners and to the fact that a marketplace viewpoint—the belief that one should commit oneself after a long process of information gathering—has pervaded romantic practices…. The affair can be viewed as a postmodern expression of *intensities* or experiences of pure sensations, desire, pleasures, non-mediated by reason, language or a master narrative of self.

Eva Illouz
"The Lost Innocence of Love: Romance as a Postmodern Condition." In *Theory, Culture & Society.* Vol. 15, Numbers 3-4. 1998.

Eclecticism is the degree zero of contemporary general culture: one listens to reggae, watches a western, eats McDonald's food for lunch and local cuisine for dinner, wears Paris perfume in Tokyo and "retro" clothes in Hong Kong; knowledge is a matter for TV games. It is easy to find a public for eclectic works. By becoming kitsch, art panders to the confusion which reigns in the "taste" of patrons. Artists, gallery owners, critics and the public wallow together in the "anything goes," and the epoch is one of slackening.

Jean-François Lyotard

Jean-François Lyotard

The Postmodern Condition: A Report on Knowledge. Minneapolis: University of Minnesota Press. 1984.

The ingredients of the postmodern self are given in three key cultural identities, those derived from the performances that define gender, social class, race and ethnicity…. These cultural identities are filtered through the personal troubles and the emotional experiences that flow from the individual's interactions with everyday life. These existential troubles look back to the dominant cultural themes of the postmodern era, including the cult of Eros, and its idealized conceptions of love and intimacy. The raw economic, racial, and sexual edges of contemporary life produce anxiety, alienation, a radical isolation from others, madness, violence, and insanity.

Norman Denzin

Images of Postmodern Society: Social Theory and Contemporary Cinema. London: Sage Publications. 1991.

[There is] one fundamental feature of all the postmodernisms … namely the effacement in them of the older (essentially high-modernist) frontier between high culture and so-called mass or commercial culture…. The postmodernisms have, in fact, been fascinated precisely by this whole "degraded" landscape of schlock and kitsch, of TV series and *Reader's Digest* culture, of advertising and motels, of the late show and the grade-B Hollywood film, of so-called paraliterature, with its airport paperback categories of the gothic and the romance, the popular biography, the murder mystery, and the science fiction or fantasy novel: materials they no longer simply "quote," as Joyce or Mahler might have done, but incorporate into their very substance… Every position on postmodernism in culture—whether apologia or stigmatization—is also at one and the same time, and necessarily, an implicitly or explicitly political stance on the nature of multinational capitalism today.

Fredric Jameson

Postmodernism or, The Cultural Logic of Late Capitalism. Durham, NC: Duke University Press. 1991.

There is less interest in constructing a coherent style than in playing with and expanding the range of familiar styles. The term style suggests coherence and hierarchical ordering of elements, some inner form and expressiveness…. It has often been argued by twentieth-century commentators that our age lacks a distinctive style. Simmel…for example, refers to the age of "no style" and Malraux…remarked that our culture is "a museum without walls"…perceptions which become heightened in postmodernism with its emphasis upon pastiche, "retro," the collapse of symbolic hierarchies, and the playback of cultures.

Mike Featherstone

Consumer Culture & Postmodernism. London: Sage Publications. 1991.

It self-consciously splices genres, attitudes, styles. It relishes the blurring or juxtaposition of forms (fiction-nonfiction), stances (straight-ironic), moods (violent-comic), cultural levels (high-low).... [I]t pulls the rug out from under itself, displaying an acute self-consciousness about the work's constructed nature. It takes pleasure in the play of surfaces, and derides the search for depth as mere nostalgia.

Todd Gitlin

"Postmodernism defined, at last!" In July/August *Utne Reader.* 1989.

Baudrillard's (1983) depiction of a postmodern simulational world is based upon the assumption that the development of commodity production couples with information technology have led to the "triumph of signifying culture"...so that social relations become saturated with shifting cultural signs to the extent that we can no longer speak of class or normativity and are faced by the "end of the social."

Mike Featherstone

"In pursuit of the postmodern: An Introduction." In M. Featherstone, ed. *Theory, Culture and Society 5.* 1988.

In general usage...modernism describes that art (not just literature) which sought to break with what had become the dominant and dominating conventions of nineteenth-century art and culture. The most important of these conventions was REALISM: the modernist artist no longer saw the highest test of his or her art as that of verisimilitude. This does not mean that all modernist art gave up the attempt to understand or represent the extra-literary world, but that it rejected those nineteenth-century standards which had hardened into unquestioned conventions.... Postmodernism, in contrast, tends to retain the relativism while abandoning the belief in the unified underlying reality.

Jeremy Hawthorn

A Concise Glossary of Contemporary Literary Theory. Third Edition. London: Arnold. 1998.

In the postmodern…Jameson…finds that pastiche, in contrast to parody, proliferates due to an "unavailability of personal style." Drawing from Michel Foucault's critique of subjectivity and Jean Baudrillard's notion of the death of the subject through an enslavement to mass-media, Jameson argues that postmodern pastiche signifies that individualism, as defined during modernism, is dead. As he asserts, "Postmodern…signals…the end of the bourgeois ego [and] the end, for example, of style, in the sense of the unique and the personal, the end of the distinctive individual brushstroke"…. Jameson thus argues that in a climate of media-enslaved, uncritical minds incapable of empowering subjectivity, pastiche thrives; postmodern uses of pastiche reflect the extent to which culture and the individual have become media-dominated.

Marci Safran

"Jameson, Jencks, and Juniors: Generation X as Critical Paradigm."
[Im]positions. Issue #1, December 1996.

Postmodern thought is characterized by a loss of belief in an objective world and an incredulity toward meta-narratives of legitimation. With a delegitimation of global systems of thought, there is no foundation to secure a universal and objective *reality*. There is today a growing public acknowledgment that "Reality isn't what it used to be"…. In philosophy there is a departure from the belief in one true reality—subjectively copied in our heads by perception or objectively represented by scientific models…. There exists no pure uninterpreted datum; all facts embody theory.

Stephen Crooks, Jan Pakulski, and Malcolm Waters

Postmodernization: Change in Advanced Society. London: Sage Publications.
1992.

Postmodernization of culture is best understood as an extension and intensification of differentiation, rationalization and commodification which dissolves the regional stability of modern culture and reverses its priorities.... Value-spheres become hyper-differentiated, that is, their internal boundaries multiply to the point of fragmentation. As the particular genre, or style, becomes the unit of production and consumption, we orient ourselves to nostalgic classicism rather than "Art," to heavy metal rather than "Music" or to nineteenth-century women novelists rather than "Literature." The eventual effect of hyperdifferentiation is to set loose cultural "fragments" of intense symbolic power which transgresses the boundaries between value-spheres and between culture and other subsystems.

Stephen Crooks, Jan Pakulski, and Malcolm Waters

Postmodernization: Change in Advanced Society. London: Sage Publications. 1992.

Media Theory

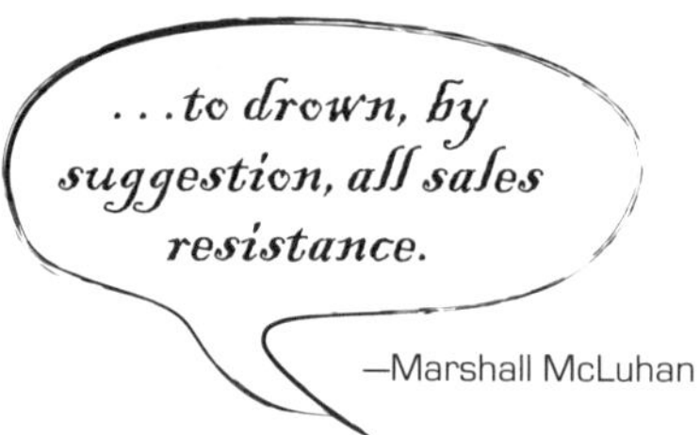

The first chapters in this book were devoted to theories and concepts from various disciplines and philosophies that can be used to analyze cultural phenomena of all kinds. This chapter, the longest in the book, focuses on various approaches to the media, which play such a large role in contemporary cultural life. For many people, the mass media are, to a great extent, their culture. Some critics use the term "mass-mediated culture," as a matter of fact.

Huge numbers of people are entertained by the media, spend enormous amounts of time with the media, shop using the media, socialize through the media (think of Twitter and Facebook), and some find their lovers on dating services using that all important new medium—the Internet. Since the media play such an important role in contemporary societies, it is only fitting that I devote a considerable amount of space to theories about the role of the media and the way they shape our consciousness. You will find many different theorists represented in this chapter, such as Marshall McLuhan, Neil Postman, Susan Sontag, and Michel de Certeau, discussing everything from photography to video games.

There is a basic principle that distinguishes a hot medium like radio from a cool one like the telephone, or a hot medium like the movie from a cool one like TV. A hot medium is one that extends one single sense in "high definition." High definition is the state of being well filled with data. A photograph is visually "high definition." A cartoon is "low definition," simply because very little visual information is provided. Telephone is a cool medium, or one of low definition, because the ear is given a meager amount of information. And speech is a cool medium of low definition, because so little is given and so much has to be filled in by the listener. On the other hand, hot media do not leave so much to be filled in or completed by the audience. Naturally, therefore, a hot medium like the radio has very different effects on the user from a cool medium like the telephone.

Marshall McLuhan

Understanding Media: *The Extensions of Man.* New York: McGraw-Hill. 1965.

There is no more disturbing consequence of the electronic and graphic revolution than this: that the world as given to us through television seems natural, not bizarre. For the loss of the sense of the strange is a sign of adjustment, and the extent to which we have adjusted is a measure of the extent to which we have changed. Our culture's adjustment to the epistemology of television is by now almost complete; we have so thoroughly accepted its definitions of truth, knowledge and reality that irrelevance seems to us to be filled with import, and incoherence seems eminently sane.

Neil Postman

Amusing Ourselves to Death: Public Discourse in the Age of Show Business. New York: Penguin. 1986.

When I fire a laser gun in a computer game such as *Space Invader,* where, and what, am "I"? Am I the sender or the receiver? I am certainly part of the medium, so perhaps I am the message. Compare Umberto Eco's statement that "what one usually calls message is rather a text a network of different messages depending on different codes...." If this definition is applied to a computer game program such as *Space Invader,* it becomes nontrivial to attribute these concepts to specific communicative positions: just as the game becomes a text for the user at the time of playing so, it can be argued, does the user become a text for the game, since they exchange and react to each other's messages according to a set of codes. The game plays the user and there is no message apart from the play.

Espen J. Aarseth

Cybertext: Perspectives on Ergodic Literature. Baltimore, MD: Johns Hopkins University Press, 1997.

First introduced on *Star Trek: The Next Generation* in 1987, the holodeck consists of an empty black cube covered in white gridlines upon which a computer can project elaborate simulations by combining holography with magnetic "force fields" and energy-to-matter conversions. The result is an illusory world that can be stopped, started, or turned off at will but that looks and behaves like the actual world and includes parlor fires, drinkable tea, and characters...who can be touched, conversed with, and even kissed. The *Star Trek* holodeck is a universal fantasy machine, open to individual programming: a vision of the computer as a kind of storytelling genie in the lamp.

Janet Murray

Hamlet on the Holodeck: The Future of Narrative in Cyberspace. Cambridge, MA: The M.I.T. Press. 1997.

Multiform stories often reflect different points of view of the same event. The classic example of this genre is *Rashomon* (1950), the Kurosawa film in which the same crime is narrated by four different people: a rape victim; her husband, who is murdered; the bandit who attacks them; and a bystander. The increasing moral confusion of their accounts in part reflects the postwar cultural crisis in Japan.

Janet Murray
Hamlet on the Holodeck: The Future of Narrative in Cyberspace. Cambridge, MA: The M.I.T. Press. 1997.

The American political scientist Harold D. Lasswell began an article in 1948 with perhaps the most famous single phrase in communication research: "A convenient way to describe an act of communication is to answer the following questions:

Who?
Says what?
In which channel?
To whom?
With what effect?"

This simple formula has been used in several ways, mostly to organize and to give structure to discussions about communication…. Lasswell himself used it to point out distinct types of communication research.

Denis McQuail and Sven Windahl
Communication Models for the Study of Mass Communication. New York: Longman. 1993.

The apparent arbitrariness of matter, in relation to the status quo of nature, is much less arbitrary than it seems. The final order is inevitably determined, consciously or unconsciously, by the social premises of the maker of the film-composition. His class-determined tendency is the basis of what seems to be an arbitrary cinematographic relation to the object placed, or found, before the camera.

Sergei Eisenstein
Film Form: Four Essays in Film Theory. Trans. Jay Leyda. Bloomington: Indiana University Press. 1949.

From our point of view, the media audience is not to be understood as mere consumers who passively accept anything that the media offer, but as active individuals and members of social groupings who consume media products in the context of their personal and social goals. In modern societies, that means quite a lot. Because the media system plays such an important role in society, linking the audience to all its various institutions, it is necessarily the case that the media will play important social and personal roles in individual and collective life.

Sandra J. Ball-Rokeach and Muriel G. Cantor
Media, Audience, and Social Structure. Thousand Oaks, CA: Sage. 1986.

Kuleshov demonstrated in class experiments that an audience's reactions to an individual shot were influenced by the shots that preceded it and followed it; that is, a cinematic narrative is constructed on the basis of a juxtaposition of related shots. Kuleshov and his associates went further. By imaginative editing and the introduction of images unrelated to but associatively connected with the narrative, they were able to generate feelings and ideas in a viewer that would not have existed without such creative editing. In short, a series of shots became more than a sum of its parts.

Dennis DeNitto
Film, Form & Feeling. New York: Harper & Row. 1985.

Photography has powers that no other image-system has ever enjoyed because, unlike the earlier ones, it is not dependent on the image maker. However carefully the photographer intervenes in setting up and guiding the image-making process, the process itself remains an optical-chemical (or electronic) one, the workings of which are automatic, the machinery for which will inevitably be modified to provide still more detailed and, therefore,

Susan Sontag

more useful maps of the real. The mechanical genesis of these images, and the literalness of the powers they confer, amounts to a new relationship between image and reality.

Susan Sontag

On Photography. New York: Farrar, Straus & Giroux. 1973.

For the first time in world history, mechanical reproduction emancipates a work of art from its parasitical dependence on ritual. To an ever greater degree, the work of art reproduced becomes the work of art designed for reproducibility. From a photographic negative, for example, one can make any number of prints; to ask for the "authentic" print makes no sense. But the instant criterion of authenticity ceases to be applicable to artistic production, the total function of art is reversed. Instead of being based on ritual, it begins to be based on another practice, politics.

Walter Benjamin

"The Work of Art in the Age of Mechanical Reproduction." In G. Mast and M. Cohen, eds. *Film Theory and criticism: Introductory readings.* Oxford: Oxford University Press. 1974.

Digital systems do not use continuously variable representational relationships. Instead, they translate all input into binary structures of Os and Is, which can then be stored, transferred, or manipulated at the level of numbers of "digits" (so called because etymologically, the word descends from the digits on our hands with which we count out those numbers).... The digital photograph, rather than being a series of tonally continuous pigmented dots, is instead composed from pixels, a grid of cells that have precise numerical attributes associated with them, a series of steps rather than a continuous slope.

Peter Lunenfeld, ed.

The Digital Dialectic: New Essays on New Media. Cambridge, MA: M.I.T. Press. 1999.

The entire study of mass communication is based on the premise that the media have significant effects, yet there is little agreement on the nature and extent of these assumed effects. This uncertainty is the more surprising since everyday experience provides countless, if minor, examples of influence. We dress for the weather as forecast, buy something because of an advertisement, go to a film mentioned in a newspaper, react in countless ways to media news, to films, to music on the radio, and so on. There are many reported cases of negative media publicity concerning, for instance, food contamination or adulteration, leading to significant changes in food consumption behaviour.

Denis McQuail

Mass Communication Theory: An Introduction. Third Edition. London: Sage Publications. 1994.

Content analysis may be defined as a methodology by which the researcher seeks to determine the manifest content of written, spoken, or published communication by *systematic, objective,* and *quantitative* analysis.... Since any written communication (and this includes novels, plays, and television scripts as well as personal letters, suicide notes, magazines, and newspaper accounts) is produced by a communicator, the *intention of the communicator* may be the object of our research. Or we may be interested in the audience, or *receiver* of the communication, and may attempt to determine something about it.

George V. Zito
Methodology and Meanings: Varieties of Sociological Inquiry. Westport, CN: Greenwood. 1975.

[On Uses and Gratifications Research] Herzog (1942) on quiz programs and the gratifications derived from listening to soap operas; Suchman (1942) on the motives for getting interested in serious music on radio; Wolfe and Fiske (1949) on the development of children's interest in comics.... Each of these investigations came up with a list of functions served either by some specific contents or some medium in question: to match one's wits against others, to get information or advice for daily living, to provide a framework for one's day, to prepare oneself culturally for the demands of upward mobility, or to be reassured about the dignity and usefulness of one's role.

E. Katz, J. G. Blumler and M. Gurevich
"Utilization of Mass Communication by the Individual." In G. Gumpert and R. Cathcart, eds. *Inter/Media.* New York: Oxford University Press. 1979.

Socially, the typographic extension of man brought in nationalism, industrialism, mass markets, and universal literacy and education. For print presented an image of repeatable precision that inspired totally new forms of extending social energies. Print released great psychic and social energies in the Renaissance, as today in Japan or Russia, by breaking the individual out of the traditional group while providing a model of how to add individual to individual in massive agglomeration of power. The same spirit of private enterprise that emboldened authors and artists to cultivate self-expression led other men to create giant corporations, both military and commercial.

Marshall McLuhan
Understanding Media: The Extensions of Man. New York: McGraw-Hill. 1965.

A genre consists of a coded set of formulas and conventions which indicate a culturally accepted way or organizing material into distinct patterns. Once established, genres dictate the basic conditions of cultural production and reception. For example, crime dramas invariably have a violent crime, a search for its perpetrators, and often a chase, fight, or bloody elimination of the criminal, communicating the message "crime does not pay." The audience comes to expect these predictable pleasures and a crime drama "code" develops, enshrined in production and studio texts and practices.

Douglas Kellner
"Television Images, Codes and Messages." *Televisions.* Vol. 7, Number 4. 1980.

The global media system is now dominated by a first tier of nine giant firms. The five largest are Time Warner (1997 sales: $24 billion), Disney ($22 billion), Bertelsmann ($15 billion), Viacom ($13 billion), and Rupert Murdoch's News Corporation ($11 billion). Besides needing global scope to compete, the rules of thumb for global media giants are twofold: First, get bigger so you dominate markets and your competition can't buy you out. Firms like Disney and Time Warner have almost tripled in size this decade. Second, have interests in numerous media industries, such as film production, book publishing, music, TV channels and networks, retail stores, amusement parks, magazines, newspapers and the like.

Robert McChesney
"The Global Media Giants." www.fair.org/extra/9711.gmg.html

In 1982, when I completed research for my book, 50 corporations controlled half or more of the media business. By December 1986, when I finished a revision for a second edition, the 50 had shrunk to 29. The last time I counted, it was down to 26. [When the latest edition of *The Media Monopoly* was published in 1993, the number was down to 20.] A number of serious Wall Street media analysts are predicting that by the 1990s, a half-dozen giant firms will control most of our media. Of the 1,700 daily papers, 98 percent are local monopolies and fewer than 15 corporations control most of the country's daily circulation. A handful of firms have most of the magazine business, with *Time* alone accounting for about 40 percent of that industry's revenues.

Ben Bagdikian

"The U.S. media: Supermarket or Assembly Line." *Journal of Communication*. Vol. 13. 1985.
www.fair.org/extra/best-of-extra/corporate-ownership.html

The medium is the message.

Marshall McLuhan

Understanding Media: The Extensions of Man. New York: McGraw-Hill. 1956.

Attraction is both socially constructed and biologically shaped to be an instantaneous decision. Whether a female is attracted to a male or vice versa is based on unconscious biological signals of sexual interest. Just as female animals are attracted to power and exhibitions of strength in males of the same species as signs of health and fertility, human females are drawn toward displays of masculine power and strength…. For females, a small waist… and a high-pitched voice are signs of vulnerability that appeal to a male's self-identification, through cultural transmission, as a protector.

Anthony J. Cortese

Provocateur: Images of Women and Minorities in Advertising. Lanham, MD: Rowman & Littlefield. 1999.

McLuhan became frustrated trying to teach first year students in required courses how to read English poetry, and began using the technique of analyzing the front page of newspapers, comic strips, ads, and the like as poems…. This new approach to the study of popular culture and popular art forms led to his first move towards new media and communication and eventually resulted in his first book, *The Mechanical Bride,* which some consider to be one of the founding documents of early cultural studies. While the *Bride* was not initially a success, it introduced one aspect of McLuhan's basic method—using poetic methods of analysis in a quasi-poetic style to analyze popular cultural phenomena—in short, assuming such cultural productions to be another type of poem.

Donald Theall

The Virtual Marshall McLuhan. Montreal and Kingston: Queen's University Press. 2001

The relationship to another's word was equally complex and ambivalent in the Middle Ages. The role of the others' word was enormous at that time: there were quotations that

M. M. Bahktin

were openly and reverently emphasized as such, or that were half-hidden, completely hidden, half-conscious, unconscious, correct, intentionally distorted, deliberately reinterpreted and so forth. The boundary lines between someone else's speech and one's own speech were flexible, ambiguous, often deliberately distorted and confused. Certain types of texts were constructed like mosaics out of the texts of others.

M. M. Bahktin

The Dialogic Imagination. Trans. Caryl Emerson and Michael Holquist. Austin, TX: University of Texas Press. 1981.

Reliable observation and systematic analysis usually require limited and objective definitions. Most research studies have defined media violence as the depiction of overt physical action that hurts or kills or threatens to do so. A terroristic act is typically defined as one involving violence by, among, or against states or other authorities in order to spread fear and make a statement, usually political. Media violence and terror are closely related. They depict social relationships and the use of force to control, dominate, provoke, or annihilate.

Nancy Signorelli and George Gerbner, eds.

Violence and Terror in the Mass Media: An Annotated Bibliography. New York: Greenwood Press. 1988.

It is a truism of our media-dominated age that television has largely usurped the traditional role of political parties. Power flows to those who control (or can afford to buy access to) the airwaves. The gatekeepers are the arbiters of visibility, such as Ted Koppel and Larry King, and their corporate media-masters; party bosses have been replaced by pollsters, media advisers, and direct-mail consultants. Virtually all political actions and communications—not just political ads but also floor speeches by legislators, news conferences, debates, and party conventions—are designed expressly for consumption as sound bites by a TV audience.

Jeffrey Scheuer

The Sound Bite Society: Television and the American Mind. New York: Four Walls Eight Windows. 1999.

There is no "mass" communication because there is no "mass" audience. Instead, there are many audiences, some with structures and leadership and others without these characteristics. Some audiences last only a few hours (Super-bowl viewers) while others last for a whole season (diehard football fans). Some audiences are based on a need for immediate information (viewers of CNN), some on in-depth information (readers of news magazines), some on a need for a religious experience (viewers of the PTL Club), some on a need for political stimulation, musical entertainment, romantic fantasy, and on and on…. Each of us is a member of multiple audiences.

W. James Potter
Media Literacy. Thousand Oaks, CA: Sage Publications. 1998.

All cultural products contain a mixture of two elements: conventions and inventions. Conventions are elements which are known to both the creator and his audience beforehand—they consists of things like favorite plots, stereotyped characters, accepted ideas, commonly known metaphors and other linguistic devices, etc. Inventions, on the other hand, are elements which are uniquely imagined by the creator such as new kinds of characters, ideas, or linguistic forms.

John Cawelti
The Six-Gun Mystique. Bowling Green, OH: The Bowling Green Popular Press. 1971.

From morning to night, narrations constantly haunt streets and buildings. They articulate our existences by teaching us what they must be. They "cover the event," that is to say, they *make* our legends (*legenda*, what is to be read and said) out of it. Captured by the radio (the voice is the law) as soon as he awakens,

Michel de Certeau

the listener walks all day long through the forest of narrativities from journalism, advertising, and television narrativities that still find time, as he is getting ready for bed, to slip a few final messages under the portals of sleep. Even more than the God told about by the theologians of earlier days, these stories have a providential and predestining function: they organize in advance our work, our celebrations, and even our dreams.

Michel de Certeau

The Practice of Everyday Life. Berkeley, CA: University of California Press. 1984.

Large pupils are sexually appealing and this dilation occurs unconsciously during arousal…. Youth is also a sign of health and sex appeal…. Women use foundation makeup to hide small wrinkles, because eliminating any signs of aging contributes toward a more desirable and attractive image. Skin tones are warmed up in order to project a healthy sexual glow.

Anthony J. Cortese

Provocateur: Images of Women and Minorities in Advertising. Lanham, MD: Rowman & Littlefield. 1999.

An exaggerated leg length appears to be more adult and, therefore, more sexual…. Hair grooming is also an important component of attraction and gender display…. A smile symbolizes approval or attraction…. Unconscious blushing is considered to be very sexual…. How female breasts are displayed is a key part of sexual attraction. The cleavage area between the breasts is perhaps the epicenter and stimulation of interest. In fact, breast cleavage and the cleavage of the buttocks are considered to be very sexual. In truth, there is a great similarity between the appearance of the two types of cleavage.

Anthony J. Cortese

Provocateur: Images of Women and Minorities in Advertising. Lanham, MD: Rowman & Littlefield. 1999.

Form of Violence	Opposite Form of Violence
1. mass mediated violence	violence we see directly
2. real mediated violence (wars)	fictive mediated violence stories
3. comic violence (kid's TV shows)	serious violence (adult films)
4. violence to individuals	violence to groups and society
5. police violence (just)	criminal violence (unjust)
6. verbal violence (insults)	physical violence (hitting someone)
7. violence to humans	violence to animals
8. "fake" violence (wrestling)	"true" violence (bar brawl)
9. violence against heroes	violence against villains
10. violence against women	violence against men
11. visual images of violence	prose descriptions of violence
12. as sign of depravity	as cry for help

Arthur Asa Berger

Essentials of Mass Communication Theory. Thousand Oaks, CA: Sage Publications. 1995.

Ad agencies are so very useful. They express for the collective that which dreams and uncensored behavior do in individuals. They give spatial form to hidden impulse and, when analyzed, make possible bringing into reasonable order a great deal that could not otherwise be observed or discussed. Gouging away at the surface of public sales resistance, the ad men are constantly breaking through into the *Alice in Wonderland* territory behind the looking glass which is the world of subrational impulse and appetites…. The ad agencies flood the daytime world of conscious purpose and control with erotic imagery from the night world in order to drown, by suggestion, all sales resistance.

Marshall McLuhan

The Mechanical Bride. Boston: Beacon Press. 1951.

Everyday media experiences are not usually at the level of a major aesthetic experience, but for many persons the most moving cultural experience will be through popular media rather than classical art. A powerful emotional experience can be triggered by an otherwise trivial song floating out an alley and awakening rich associations. The important quality in the aesthetic experience, whether it is an emotional, earthshaking, life-changing encounter or a quiet, simple, weightless sense of deep appreciation is your subjective response.

Michael R. Real

Exploring Media Culture: A Guide. Thousand Oaks: CA: Sage Publications. 1996.

Narrative is the primary way through which humans organize their experiences into temporally meaningful episodes…. Narrative is both a mode of reasoning and a mode of representation. People can "apprehend" the world narratively and people can "tell" about the world narratively. According to Jerome Bruner…narrative reasoning is one of the two basic and universal human cognition modes. The other mode is the logico-scientific…the logico-scientific mode looks for universal truth conditions, whereas the narrative mode looks for particular connections between events.

Laurel Richardson

"Narrative and Sociology." *Journal of Contemporary Ethnology.* Vol. 19, No. 1. April 1990.

Video games have auto-erotic aspects to them, as the term "joy stick" suggests. Marshall McLuhan argued that electronic media should be seen as extensions of ourselves "outside of our bodies." Thus, when we play these games, we are, in a way, playing with ourselves. I don't think I'm stretching the truth too far to suggest that these games have aspects of them that can be seen as a disguised form of electronic masturbation. In *Pac Man*, the violence is feminized and is based on biting and ingestion rather than shooting guns and rockets off and other masculine and phallic forms of violence and aggression. This gobbling of dots reflects a feminized form of aggression and is regressive. From a developmental standpoint, we have regressed from our phallic, gun-shooting stage (*Space Invaders*) to a more infantile oral stage.

Arthur Asa Berger

"Pac-Man: Auto-Erotic Plaything." *Los Angeles Times*. May 2, 1984.

Advertisements sanctify, signify, mythologize, and fantasize. They uphold some of the existing economic and political structures and subvert others. Not only does advertising shape American culture; it shapes Americans' images of themselves.

Katherine Toland Frith, ed.

Undressing the Ad: Reading Culture in Advertising. New York: Peter Lang. 1997.

Advertising transfers its breadth of experience and calculation to its target groups. It treats its human targets like commodities, to whom it offers the solution to their problem of realization. Clothes are advertised like packaging as a means of sales promotion. This is one of the many ways in which commodity aesthetics takes possession of people. The two central areas in which advertising offers, by means of commodities, to solve the problems of "scoring hits" and sales are, on the one hand, following a career of the labour market and, on the other, gaining the respect of and attracting others.

W. F. Haug

Critique of Commodity Aesthetics: Appearance, Sexuality and Advertising in Capitalist Society. Minneapolis: University of Minnesota Press. 1986.

A woman whose romance has failed and who is looking for a new partner was recommended by *Teen* magazine in 1969, as "step 9" in its advice, to "become overwhelmingly pretty…. Why not try what you've never tried before? If you want to scour the market, you've got to show yourself in your best packaging." Where love succeeds, brought about by this fashionable packaging, and leads to encounters which under existing conditions appear in the form of a commodity-cash nexus, the cost of clothes can be interpreted as "capital investment."

W. F. Haug

Critique of Commodity Aesthetics: Appearance, Sexuality and Advertising in Capitalist Society. Minneapolis: University of Minnesota Press. 1986.

The most important effects of this powerful institution are not upon the economics of our distributive system; they are upon the values of our society. If the economic effect is to make the purchaser like what he buys, the social effect is, in a parallel but broader sense, to make the individual like what he gets— to enforce already existing attitudes, to diminish the range and variety of choices, and in terms of abundance, to exalt the materialistic virtues of consumption.

David Potter

People of Plenty: Economic Abundance and American Character. Chicago: University of Chicago Press. 1954.

Department Store	**Cathedral**
Modern	Medieval
Paradisical: Heaven on Earth Now	Paradisical: Heaven in the Future
Passion: Merchandising	Passion: Salvation
Sales: Save Money	Prayer: Save Souls
Sacred Texts: Catalogs	Sacred Texts: Bible, Prayer Books
Clerks	Clergy
Sell: Products	Sell: God
Possessions as Signs of Spiritual Election	Holiness as a Sign of Spiritual Election
Big Sales	Religious Holidays
Sale of an Expensive Product	Conversion of a Sinner
Buy Incredible Gifts	Experience Miracles
Pay Taxes	Pay Tithe
Muzac	Religious Music
Lighting to Sell	Lighting to Inspire Reverence
Bad Credit	Penance
Advertising	Proselytizing
Cash Register	Offering Plate
Brand Loyalty	Devotion

Arthur Asa Berger

Ads, Fads and Consumer Culture. Third Edition. Lanham, MD: Rowman & Littlefield. 2007.

When we think of those phenomena in which mimicry is likely to play a role, we enumerate such things as dress, mannerisms, facial expressions, speech, stage acting, artistic creation, and so forth. Consequently, we see imitation in social life as a force for gregariousness and bland conformity through the mass reproduction of a few social models. If imitation also plays a role in desire, if it contaminates our urge to acquire and possess, this conventional view, while not entirely false, misses the main point. Imitation does not merely draw people together, it pulls them apart. Paradoxically, it can do these two things simultaneously. Individuals who desire the same thing are united by something so powerful that, as long as they can share whatever they desire, they remain the best of friends; as soon as they cannot, they become the worst of enemies.

René Girard

A Theater of Envy: William Shakespeare. New York: Oxford University Press. 1991.

For the semiotician, the contradictory nature of the American myth of equality is nowhere written so clearly as in the signs that American advertisers use to manipulate us into buying their wares. "Manipulate" is the word here, not "persuade"; for advertising campaigns are not sources of product information, they are exercises in behavior modification. Appealing to our subconscious emotions rather than to our conscious intellects, advertisements are designed to exploit the discontentment fostered by the American dream, the constant desire for social success and the material rewards that accompany it. America's consumer economy runs on desire, and advertising stokes the engines by transforming common objects—from peanut butter to political candidates—into signs of all the things that Americans covet most.

Jack Solomon

The Signs of Our Times: The Secret Meanings of Everyday Life. New York: Perennial. 1990.

Whether we are considering ordinary conversation, a public speech, a letter, or a poem, we always find a *message* which proceeds from a *sender* to a *receiver.* These are the most obvious aspects of communication. But a successful communication depends on three other aspects of the event as well: the message must be delivered through a *contact,* physical and/or psychological; it must be framed in a *code;* and it must refer to a *context.* In the area of context, we find what a message is about. But to get there we must understand the code in which the message is framed—as in the present case, my messages reach you through the medium of an academic/literary subcode of the English language. And even if we have the code, we understand nothing until we make contact with the utterance; in the present case, until you see the printed words on this page (or hear them read aloud) they do not exist as a message for you.

Robert Scholes

Structuralism: An Introduction. New Haven, CN: Yale University Press. 1974.

The National Association of Broadcasters' Television Code limits the number of commercials permitted on television to 9.5 minutes an hour during prime time and 16 minutes an hour during other times, except during children's programming, which is more limited. Since the currently preferred length of a single TV spot is 30 seconds, the number of spots per hour averages from 19 to 32. The largest percentage of television viewing occurs during prime time, but if we average 19 and 32, we arrive at a figure of 25.5 spots per hour. On the average, each American sees 156 spots a day, or 1,092 spots a week. One hour and 18 minutes of the average American's daily television viewing consists of television spots, or about nine hours and six minutes a week.

Bruce Kurtz

Spots: The Popular Art of American Television Commercials. New York: Arts Communications. 1977.

Henri Lefebvre

In the second half of the twentieth century in Europe, or at any rate in France, there is *nothing*—whether object, individual, or social group—that is *valued* apart from its double, the image that advertises and sanctifies it. This image *duplicates* not only an object's material, perceptible existence but desire and pleasure that it makes into fictions situating them in the land of make-believe, promising "happiness"—the happiness of being a consumer. Thus publicity [advertising] that was intended to promote consumption is the first of consumer goods; it creates myths—or since it can create nothing—it borrows existing myths, canalizing signifiers to a dual purpose: to offer them as such for general consumption and to stimulate the consumption of a specific object.

Henri Lefebvre

Everyday Life in the Modern World. New Brunswick, NJ: Transaction Publications. 1984.

The knowingness and scepticism of advertising audiences are now taken for granted by advertising professionals and media studies analysts…. The knowledge of the audience, and their indifference, pose problems both for the advertisers and for analysts of advertising. For the advertisers, the problem is getting around the scepticism, the knowingness, and the boredom, and still having an effect, or even using these responses for their own purposes. For the analysts, the scepticism and knowingness undermine simplistic critiques of advertising effects, in which people do what ads tell them, accept the roles offered in ads as representations of the world, and take up the positions offered by advertising texts. But if they know how advertising works, does this protect them against its effects? Or is their knowingness limited and ultimately deceptive?

Greg Myers

Ad Worlds: Brands/Media/Audiences. London: Arnold. 1999.

The basis of modern media effectiveness is a language within a language—one that communicates to each of us at a level beneath our conscious awareness, one that reaches into the uncharted mechanism of the human unconscious. This is a language based upon the human ability to *subliminally* or *subconsciously* or *unconsciously* perceive information. This is a language that today has actually produced the profit base for North American mass communication media. It is virtually impossible to pick up a newspaper or magazine, turn on a radio or television set, read a promotional pamphlet or the telephone book, or shop through a supermarket without having your subconscious purposely massaged by some monstrously clever artist, photographer, writer, or technician.

Wilson Bryan Key

Subliminal Seduction. New York: Signet. 1973.

Do television commercials make people behave like Pavlov's dogs? Coca-Cola Co. says the answer is yes. In recent years the Atlanta soft-drink company has been refining an ad-testing procedure based on the behavioral principles developed by the Russian physiologist. So far, Coke says, its new testing system has worked remarkably well. In his classic experiment, Ivan Pavlov discovered he could get dogs to salivate at the ring of a bell by gradually substituting the sound for a spray of meat powder. Coca-Cola says that, just as Pavlov's dogs began to associate a new meaning with the bell, advertising is supposed to provide some new image or meaning for a product.

"Coca-Cola Turns to Pavlov...." *The Wall Street Journal.* January 19, 1984.

Although the specifics of Coke's test are a secret, the company says it attempts to evaluate how well a commercial "conditions" a viewer to accept a positive image that can be transferred to the product. During the past three years, Coca-Cola says, ads that scored well in its tests almost always resulted in higher sales of soft drinks. "We nominate Pavlov as the father of modern advertising," says Joel S. Dubrow, communications research manager at Coke. "Pavlov took a neutral object and, by associating it with a meaningful object, made it a symbol of something else; he imbued it with imagery, he gave it added value." That, says Mr. Dubrow, "is what we try to do with modern advertising."

"Coca-Cola Turns to Pavlov...." *The Wall Street Journal.* January 19, 1984.

Advertisers have an enormous financial stake in a narrow ideal of femininity that they promote, especially in beauty product ads.... The image of the beautiful woman...may perhaps be captured with the concept of the *perfect provocateur* (an ideal image that arouses a feeling or reaction). The exemplary female prototype in advertising, regardless of product or service, displays youth (no lines or wrinkles), good looks, sexual seductiveness... and perfection (no scars, blemishes, or even pores).... The perfect provocateur is not human; rather, she is a form or hollow shell representing a female figure. Accepted attractiveness is her only attribute. She is slender, typically tall and long-legged. Women are constantly held to this unrealistic standard of beauty. If they fail to attain it, they are led to feel guilty and ashamed. Cultural ideology tells women that they will not be desirable to, or loved by, men unless they are physically perfect.

Anthony J. Cortese

Provocateur: Images of Women and Minorities in Advertising. Second Edition. Lanham, MD: Rowman & Littlefield. 2004.

Because she is the emblem of spending ability and the chief spender, she is also the most effective seller of this world's goods. Every survey has shown that the image of an attractive woman is the most effective advertising gimmick. She may sit astride the mudguard of a new car, or step into it ablaze with jewels; she may lie at a man's feet stroking his new socks; she may hold the petrol pump in a challenging pose, or dance through the woodland glades in slow motion in all the glory of a new shampoo; whatever she does her image sells.

Germaine Greer

The Female Eunuch. New York: McGraw-Hill. 1971.

The movies, television, magazine and newspaper ads, posters, store-window mannequins, life-size, smaller than life, bigger than life, in colors or in black-and-white, in partial or total undress, in all kinds of alluring and enticing positions with the most express indications of availability, willingness, readiness to welcome you into their arms... have the combined and cumulative effect of making many men dissatisfied with whatever sexual activity is available to them.

Raphael Patai

Myth and Modern Man. Englewood Cliffs, NJ: Prentice-Hall. 1972.

His long straight snout bulges from above two pouchy folds as he stares insouciantly out at the viewer, a lighted cigarette

Marjorie Garber

hanging from his lips. Look again. Any schoolchild can recognize this ribald caricature; only adults need to have it pointed out.

Marjorie Garber
"Joe Camel, an X-Rated Smoke." *The New York Times*. March. 20, 1992.

The sexual explicitness of contemporary advertising is a sign not so much of American sexual fantasies as of the lengths to which advertisers will go to get attention. Sex never fails as an attention-getter, and in a particularly competitive and expansive era for American marketing, advertisers like to bet on a sure thing. Ad people refer to the proliferation of TV, radio, newspaper, magazine, and billboard ads as "clutter," and nothing cuts through clutter like sex. By showing the flesh, advertisers work on the deepest, most coercive human emotions of all. Much sexual coercion in advertising, however, is a sign of a desperate need to make certain that clients are getting their money's worth.

Jack Solomon
The Signs of Our Times: The Secret Meanings of Everyday Life. New York: Perennial. 1990.

The effect of advertiser-driven campaigning has been felt in more than just the professionalization of electoral propaganda, though the slickly produced political advertisement is certainly its most visible product. Promotion has been drawn into the heart of the process. Through the 1970s and 1980s it has become normal practice for the managers of campaign advertising to be recruited directly from the highest ranks of the advertising industry. Their role, moreover, sometimes in collision with the official party machine, has been not just to supervise the specifics of advertising, but to map out entire campaigns. The scope for involvement is endless. Every public statement or gesture by campaigners, whether intentional or not, can be considered part of the campaign, and is therefore susceptible to promotional orchestration.

Andrew Wernick

Promotional Culture: Advertising, Ideology and Symbolic Expression. London: Sage. 1991.

Under the heading of deceptive editing of "documentary" material, we might also want to consider a notorious political ad used in Richard Nixon's 1968 presidential campaign. Aired only once, the ad juxtaposed images of Nixon's Democratic opponent, Hubert Humphrey, with scenes of warfare in Vietnam, protests in the streets of Chicago, and poverty in Appalachia. Because Humphrey was smiling in some of the shots, these juxtapositions created the impression that he was indifferent to the suffering and disturbances in the other images.

Paul Messaris

Visual Persuasion: The Role of Images in Advertising. Thousand Oaks, CA: Sage. 1997.

If we were to sum up the total number of product advertisements we are exposed to on TV, radio, newspapers and magazines, the number could be as high as 400 per day…. If we were to add up *all* promotional messages—including logos on products, program promos and ads on billboards (two media that carry nothing but advertisements)—this number could reach 16,000…. Jacobson and Mazur…argue that typical Americans will spend almost 3 whole years of their lives just watching commercials on television. The United States, in fact, is ad burdened. This country accounts for 57% of the world's advertising spending, yet the U.S. population makes up less than 10% of the world's population.

Matthew P. McAllister

The Commercialization of American Culture: New Advertising, Control and Democracy. Thousand Oaks, CA: Sage Publications. 1996.

All of us, no matter how irresolute we are, like to think that we reign supreme in our own consciousness, that we are masters of what our minds accept or reject. Since the Soul is not much mentioned any more, except by priests, poets, and pop musicians, the last refuge a man can take from the catastrophic world at large seems be his own mind. Where else can he expect to withstand the daily siege, if not within himself? Even under the conditions of totalitarian rule, where no one can fancy any more that his home is his castle, the mind of the individual is considered a kind of last citadel and hotly defended, though this imaginary fortress may have been long since taken over by an ingenious enemy. No illusion is more stubbornly upheld than the sovereignty of the mind. It is a good example of the impact of philosophy on people who ignore it; for the idea that men can "make up their minds" individually and by themselves is essentially derived from the tenets of bourgeois philosophy.

Hans Magnus Enzenberger
The Consciousness Industry. On Literature, Politics, and the Media. New York: Seabury. 1974.

This indispensable handbook describes 4-to-12 year olds as having the greatest sales potential of any age or demographic group. Each year, children spend over $9 billion of their own money; they influence $130 billion of adults' spending; and as future adult customers, they will control even more purchasing dollars tomorrow.

Kids as Customer. November catalogue. *Marketing Power: The Marketer's Reference Library.* 1995.

Culture is a paradoxical commodity. So completely is it subject to the law of exchange that it is no longer exchanged; it is so blindly consumed in use that it can no longer be used. Therefore it amalgamates with advertising. The more meaningless the latter seems to be under a monopoly, the more omnipotent it becomes.

The motives are markedly economic. One could certainly live without the culture industry, therefore it necessarily creates too much satiation and apathy. In itself, it has few resources itself to correct this. Advertising is its elixir of life.

Max Horkheimer and Theodor W. Adorno
The Dialectics of Enlightenment. New York: Continuum. 1995.

Under monopoly all mass culture is identical, and the lines of its artificial framework begin to show through. The people at the top are no longer so interested in concealing monopoly: as its violence becomes more open, so its power grows. Movies and radio need no longer pretend to be art. The truth is that they are just business is made into an ideology to justify the rubbish they deliberately produce.

Max Horkheimer and Theodor W. Adorno
The Dialectics of Enlightenment. New York: Continuum. 1995.

[Dan] Nichols' McDonald's spots possess the most accelerated time sense of any on television. "Quick Cuts" contains more cuts than can be counted: after repeated views the author had to slow down the tape to count 65 different scenes in 60 seconds. A seven-second segment of this spot contains fourteen separate scenes, or two per second. Incredible as it may seem, it *is* possible for the viewer to perceive these different scenes even though they go by faster than they can be counted.

Bruce Kurtz
Spots: The Popular Art of American Television Commercials. New York: Arts Communication. 1977.

The effect on the viewer is a sense of extreme urgency and of the present tense: the action is thrust into the immediate present because it is rendered as more alive and exciting than even the most engaging real-life experience. Nichols taps the "live" associations of television in this way more insistently than any other director. Because of the sense of urgency and of presentness which the spots communicate, the viewer actually experiences the exciting life style which Nichols depicts rather than passively observing events which occur to someone else. The excitement communicated by the way of life the viewer thus experiences is associated with the product even though the product is not the primary subject of the spots.

Bruce Kurtz

Spots: The Popular Art of American Television Commercials. New York: Arts Communication. 1977.

Beyond attracting the viewer's attention, the image(s) in an ad are typically meant to give rise to some emotional disposition toward the product, politician, social cause, or whatever else the ad is about. The iconicity of visual images serves this process by making it possible for images to draw upon the rich variety of visual stimuli and associated emotions to which we a re already attuned through our interactions with our social and natural environments: facial expressions, gestures, postures, personal appearance, physical surroundings, and so on. Moreover…visual images are capable of simulating certain aspects of these interactions by means of the variables that control the viewer's perspective: degree of proximity, angle of view, presence of absence of subjective shots, and so on.

Paul Messaris

Visual Persuasion: The Role of Images in Advertising. Thousand Oaks, CA: Sage Publications. 1997.

The tendency to interpret *everything* in an artistic text as meaningful is so great that we rightfully consider nothing accidental in a work of art…. Since it can concentrate a tremendous amount of information into the "area" of a very small text… an artistic textmanifests

Yuri Lotman

yet another feature: it transmits different information to different readers in proportion to each one's comprehension; it provides the reader with a language in which each successive portion of information may be assimilated with repeated reading. It behaves as a kind of living organism which has a feedback channel to the reader and thereby instructs him.

Yuri Lotman

The Structure of the Artistic Texts. Trans. G. Lenhoff and R. Vroon. Ann Arbor: Michigan Slavic Contributions. 1977.

A number of years ago I developed a myth model that suggested, in essence, that many of the things we do in the contemporary world—or maybe the contemporary secular world would be more accurate—are really tied in curious and interesting ways to ancient myths. Or to be a bit more precise many of our activities are desacralized manifestations of ancient myths. We have emptied the religious content out of the myths and don't even recognize that what we are doing is, vaguely speaking, a ritual tied to a myth. The myth model attempts to show how ancient myths inform many contemporary activities, whose relation to these myths is beyond our awareness.

Myth	Medusa
Historical Act	Cleopatra kills herself with an asp
Elite Culture Text	Shakespeare: *Antony and Cleopatra*
Popular Culture Text	Fidji "Woman with Snake" advertisement
Everyday Life	Woman dabs on Fidji perfume

Arthur Asa Berger

Ads, Fads and Consumer Culture. Third Edition. Lanham, MD: Rowman & Littlefield. 2007

Some measure of greed exists unconsciously in everyone. It represents an aspect of the desire to live, one which is mingled and fused at the outset of life with the impulse to turn aggression and destructiveness outside ourselves against others, and as such it persists unconsciously throughout life. By its very nature it is endless and never assuaged; and being a form of the impulse to live, it ceases only with death. The longing or greed for good things can relate to any and every imaginable kind of good—material possessions, bodily or mental gifts, advantages and privileges; but, beside the actual gratifications they may bring, in the depths of our minds they ultimately signify one thing. They stand as proofs to us, if we get them, that we are ourselves good, and full of good, and so are worthy of love, or respect and honour, in return.

Joan Riviere

"Hate, Greed and Aggression." In Melanie Klein and Joan Riviere. *Love, Hate and Reparation.* New York: Norton. 1967.

To manufacture a product without at the same time manufacturing a demand has become unthinkable. Today the manufacture of demand means, for most large companies, television—its commercials as well as other program elements. The growing scale of mass production has inevitably made advertising more crucial, but this understates the situation. As society becomes more product-glutted, the pressure on the consumer to consume—to live up to higher and higher norms of consumption—has become unrelenting.

Erik Barnouw

The Sponsor: Notes on a Modern Potentate. New York: Oxford University Press. 1979.

The pressure, as various observers have noted, centers on selling the unnecessary. The merchandising of necessities—which, to some extent, will be bought anyway—can seldom sustain the budgets applied to the unnecessary, unless the necessary is cloaked with mythical supplemental values. The focus is on the creation of emotion-charged values to make the unneeded necessary. All this is now so taken for granted that it is seldom discussed. The young writer entering advertising assumes that hope and fear are the springs he must touch—hope of success and fear of failure in sex, business, community status. As a dramatic medium that can draw on the resources of every art, and has as its stage the privacy of the home, television has unparalleled opportunity for this psychic pressure.

Erik Barnouw

The Sponsor: Notes on a Modern Potentate. New York: Oxford University Press. 1979.

Postmodern advertising—characterized by a rapid succession of visually appealing images (the speed-up effect), repetition, and high-volume, mood-setting music...is much more symbolic and persuasive than informative. Advertising is an arena in which conspicuous role display and reversal, preening, and symbolically enticing situations are evident.... While modern advertising presented itself as an unquestionable authority figure—a high priest of sorts—postmodern advertising presents itself as an insider, an ally of the common person. Modern advertising uses a paternalistic model; like your physician, it knows what is best for you. Now advertising is trading in the semblance of god-like knowledge for the role of a funny, self-deprecatory chum.

Anthony J. Cortese

Provocateur: Images of Women and Minorities in Advertising. Second Edition. Lanham, MD: Rowman & Littlefield. 2004.

Every extra-artistic prose discourse—in any of its forms, quotidian, rhetorical, scholarly—cannot fail to be oriented toward the "already uttered," the "already known," the "common opinion" and so forth. The dialogic orientation of discourse is a phenomenon that is, of course, a property of *any* discourse... .[E]very word is directed toward an *answer* and cannot escape the profound influence of the answering world that it anticipates. The word in living conversation is directly, blatantly, oriented toward a future answer-word: it provokes an answer, anticipates it and structures itself in the atmosphere of the already spoken, the word is at the same time determined by that which has not been said but which is needed and in fact anticipated by the answering world. Such is the situation in any dialogue.

Mikhail Bakhtin

The Dialogic Imagination. Michael Holquist, ed. Trans. Caryl Emerson and Michael Holquist. Austin, TX: University of Texas Press. 1981.

Today we celebrate the first glorious anniversary of the information purification repentance. We who created from out of this time in all history a garden of pure ideology, where each worker may loom secure from the pest of purveying contradictory thoughts. Our communication is enormous. It is more powerful than any fleet or army on earth. We are one people with one will, one resolve, one cause. Our enemies shall talk themselves to death and we will bury them with their own confusion. We shall prevail... [At this point television screen is shattered]

Macintosh 1984 commercial.

In terms of the big question, there is rather high agreement between the student respondents and the critic and creator on the element of the message that focuses on the introduction of the Macintosh computer. This is particularly important since advertising researchers know that the miscomprehension rate of television advertising message points is close to 25 percent. Other elements which the creator and critic thought were important message points were rarely or barely noted, which suggests that a deep reading from a fleeting exposure to a television commercial is probably not realistic... .While the *1984* story line was extremely powerful, the Macintosh message was still the focus of their interpretations. While in slightly more than half the cases they were reading and interpreting the stories at a simple level, the number that engaged in a more elaborate decoding with some interpretation beyond simply re-telling was higher than the researchers expected almost reaching 50 percent. This suggests that viewers of a fast paced, complex commercial may be able to engage in sophisticated interpretation even from a brief exposure.

Sandra Moriarty and Shay Sayre
"A Comparison of Reader Response with Informed Author/Viewer Analysis." Unpublished paper. 1991.

The real significance of advertising is its total cumulative weight as part of the culture—in the way in which it contributes to the popular lore of ideas and attitudes towards consumer products. The information and impressions which people have about branded goods represent folk wisdom: they are part of the landscape of symbols with which people are familiar from childhood on, and which they play back to each other in the discussions that precede a major purchase.

Leo Bogart
Strategy in Advertising. New York: Harcourt Brace. 1967.

On the most obvious level television is a dramatic medium simply because a large proportion of the material it transmits is in the form of traditional drama, consisting of fictional material mimetically represented by actors and employing plot, dialogue, character, gesture, costume—the whole panoply of dramatic means of expression....The time devoted by the average American adult male to watching dramatic material on television thus accounts to over 12 hours per week, while the average American woman sees almost 16 hours of drama on television each week. That means that the average American adult sees the equivalent of *five to six full-length stage plays a week*!

Martin Esslin
The Age of Television. San Francisco, CA: W. H. Freeman. 1982.

Audiences not only learn about public issues and other matters from the media, they also learn how much *importance* to attach to an issue or topic from the emphasis the media put on it.

Maxwell E. McCombs and Donald L. Shaw
"Structuring the 'Unseen Environment.'" *Journal of Communication*. 26, 2. Spring 1976.

What is the world according to television like? To discover its main features and functions, we have to look at familiar structures in an unfamiliar light. Rituals rationalize and serve a social order. They make the necessary and inevitable appear natural and right. In conventional entertainment stories, plots perform that rationalizing function. They provide novelty, diversion, and distraction from the constant reiteration of the functions performed by casting, power, and fate. The main points to observe, therefore, are who is who (number and characterization of different social types in the cast); who risks and gets what (power to allocate resources including personal integrity, freedom of action, and safety); and who comes to what end (fate, or outcomes inherent in the structure that relates social types to a calculus of power, risks and relative success or failure).

George Gerbner
Journal of Communication. Spring 1974.

[Jonathan] Edwards argues that all acts of will, like events in physical nature, are subject to the law of causation. Since an act of will has its cause in a previous act of will, and this in turn in an earlier one, we must eventually arrive at a first act, which was necessarily caused by the agent's inborn disposition. Having traced the whole series backward to the start, we come to realize that the will has no independent activity but is merely passive and mechanical. Man does have freedom, to be sure, in the sense that he feels no compulsion or restraint but can "do as he pleases." Yet his will cannot determine *what* he pleases to do. He is free to *act* as he chooses, but has no *freedom of choice.*

Norman Foerster, ed.

American Poetry & Prose, Part One. Fourth Edition. Boston: Houghton Mifflin. 1957.

Coda

This book contains approximately three hundred quotations from the most important thinkers whose theories and concepts are used by practitioners of cultural studies. I've selected quotations that I have used over the years and that other cultural critics use, as well. You have, in this book, a repertoire of concepts that you can use when you are investigating some topic, for an article, a term paper, or to satisfy your curiosity. In the course of my career as a professor I've met many students who had never read any Freud, Marx, Saussure, Durkheim or any of the other important thinkers quoted in this book. This book will help remedy that deficiency in all who read it.

In the course of my career, a number of people have asked me how I was able to publish more than sixty books. I've actually written more books but not all of them have been published. I generally tell them that I know some theories and have learned how to apply the concepts found in these theories to any number of different topics. It is through theories and concepts that I make sense of things that interest me. When I have some topic that I want to write about, in my mind I think "round up the usual suspects," and then I see what ideas these "suspects" (cultural studies theorists) have to offer that I can use. It also helps if you know how to type with ten fingers and are disciplined.

About the Author

Arthur Asa Berger is professor emeritus of Broadcast and Electronic Communication Arts at San Francisco State University, where he taught between 1965 and 2003. He is the author of more than one hundred articles published in the United States and abroad, numerous book reviews, and more than 60 books on the mass media, popular culture, humor, and everyday life. Among his books are *Media Analysis Techniques* (3rd edition), *Media & Society* (2nd edition), *Seeing is Believing: An Introduction to Visual Communication* (3rd edition), *Ads, Fads And Consumer Culture* (3rd edition), *and Shop 'Til You Drop: Consumer Behavior and American Culture.*

He has also written a number of comic academic mysteries such as *Postmortem for a Postmodernist, The Hamlet Case, Mistake in Identity, The Mass Comm Murders: Five Media Theorists Self-Destruct,* and *Durkheim is Dead: Sherlock Holmes is Introduced to Sociological Theory.* His books have been translated into German, Italian, Russian, Arabic, Swedish, Korean, Turkish and Chinese, and he has lectured in more than a dozen countries in the course of his career.

Berger is married, has two children and four grandchildren, and lives in Mill Valley, California. He enjoys travel and dining in ethnic restaurants. He also lectures on cruise ships about media and popular culture. He can be reached by e-mail at: arthurasaberger@gmail.com.